Good Day

Poetry & Images for Seasons of Optimism

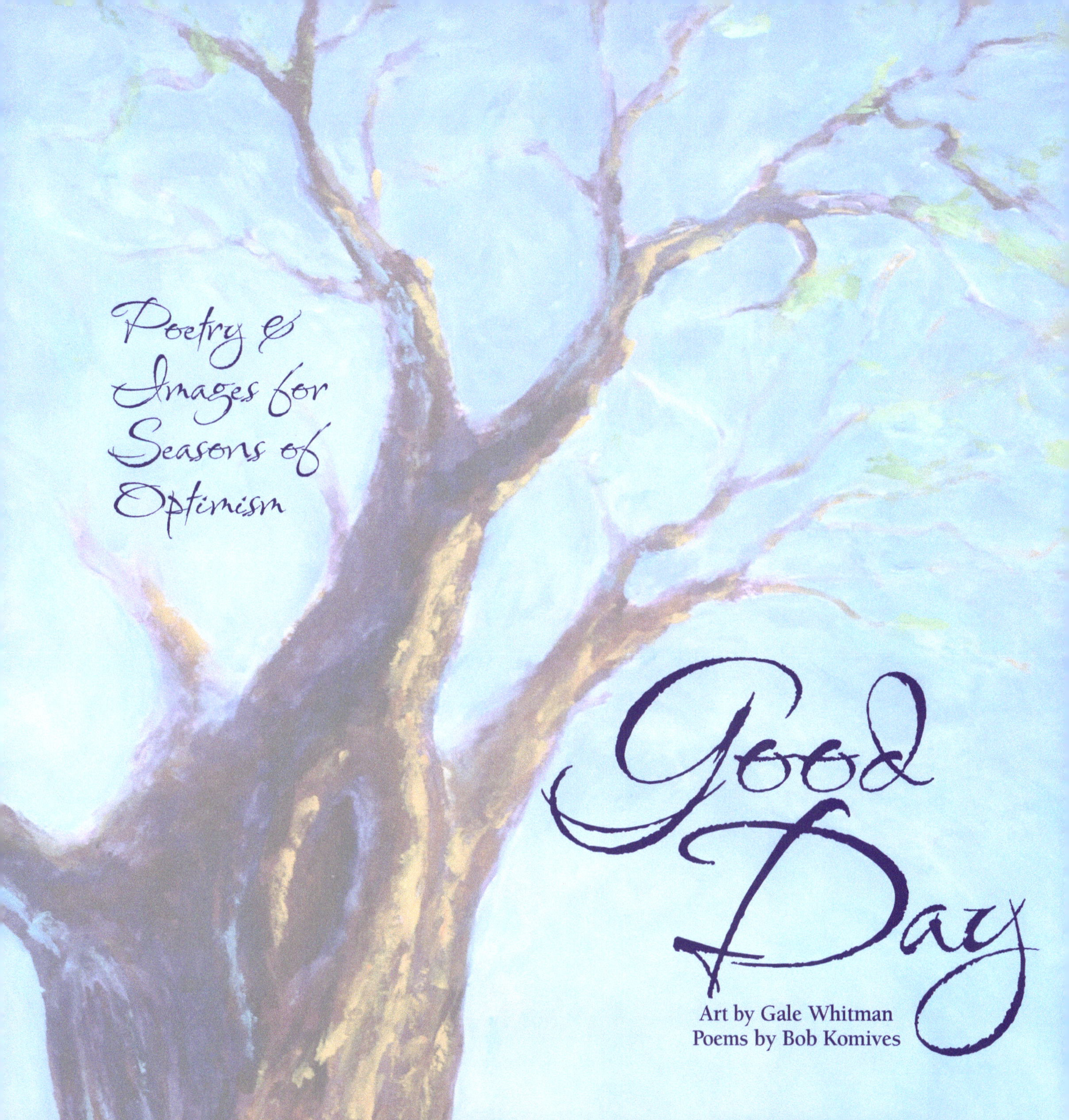

Poetry &
Images for
Seasons of
Optimism
Good
Day
Art by Gale Whitman
Poems by Bob Komives

Good Day

Poetry & Images for Seasons of Optimism

Second Edition

ISBN: 978-0-9629281-8-5

Published in the United States of America, 2018, by RPK Press, Fort Collins.

For information, contact Komives-Whitman at RPK Press at 324 East Plum Street, Fort Collins, Colorado 80524

Book design: Becky Hawley Design

Photos of artwork: Robert Campagna Photography

Cover: Seasoned Optimism (detail)

Pages 8–9: Sun on Their Faces

RPK Press
Komives-Whitman
324 East Plum Street
Fort Collins, CO 80524

www.GoodDayArtPoetry.com

The book you hold in your hand is the collaborative expression of two who are friends and neighbors—a poet and an artist. The artistic expressions of each inspire the other, all within a supportive community. Gale, the painter, and Bob, the poet, are optimists who struggle in their lives and arts to remain optimistic and to foster optimism in others who share their hopes and concerns. For this is another era in the history of our imperfect species when we seem at times and places to act against ourselves and the earth that sustains us. Each generation must take up the challenge to do more good than harm. It is our turn, Bob and Gale's turn as artists, to save, beautify, improve and enjoy this bountiful and troubled world. It is tempting to wallow in despair, but, as Bob and Gale like to say: every depressing hour calls out for the creative day! That call gives birth to this book of mutually inspired words and paintings.

Inebriation by Optimism

There was to be mist and then sunshine,
but we worked dry all day under cloud.
All morning
we seeded hope's anticipation.
After noon,
weeded patches of doubt.
They predict no rain for tomorrow;
we may stand dry again without sun.
Yet, as we relax together this evening
(weary and worried for our work)
we sip from good harvest past.
We rise in lightness and confidence.
We speak of sun and rainfall to come.
With few hours to enjoy before sleeping,
inebriation by optimism has begun.

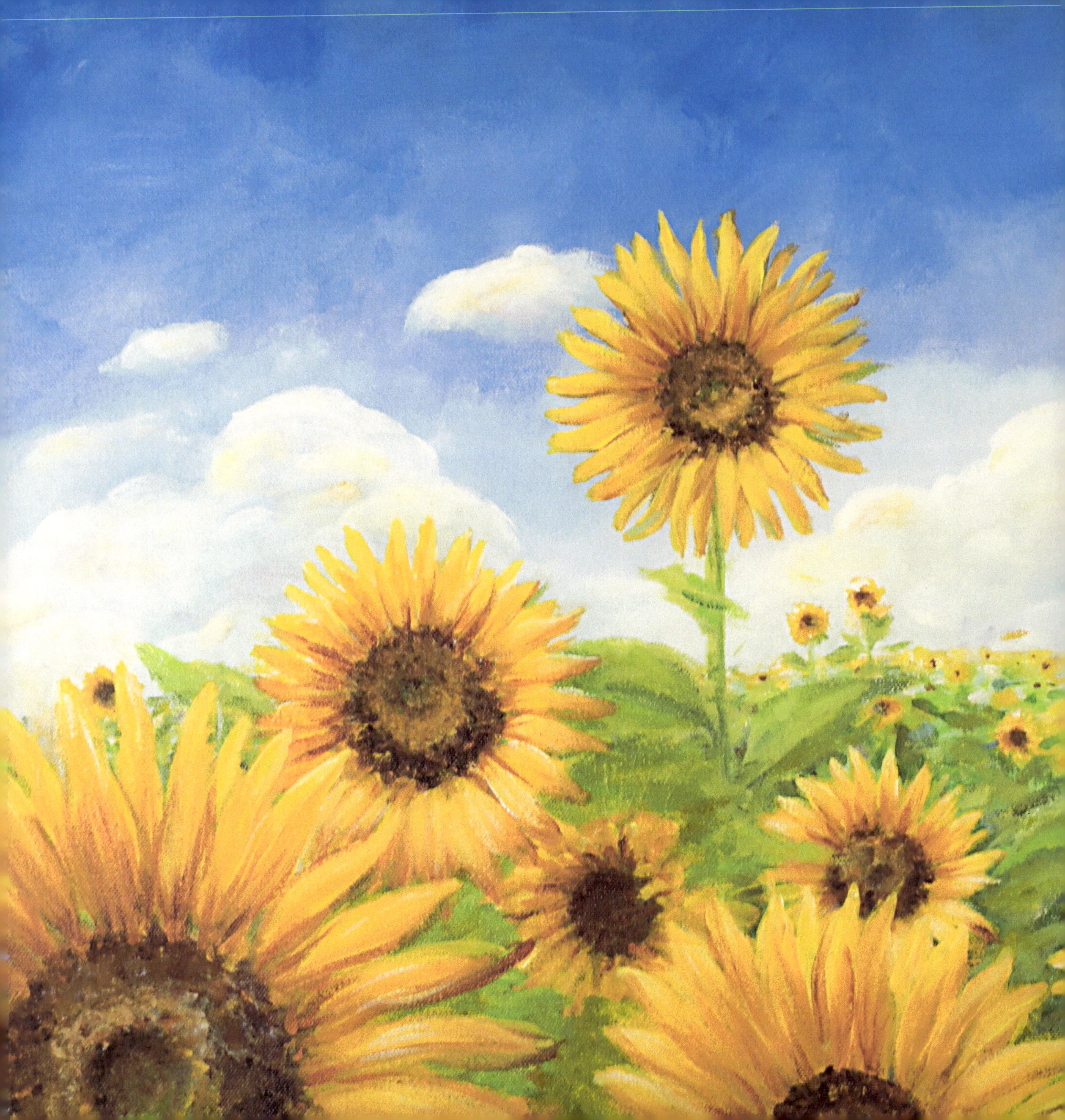

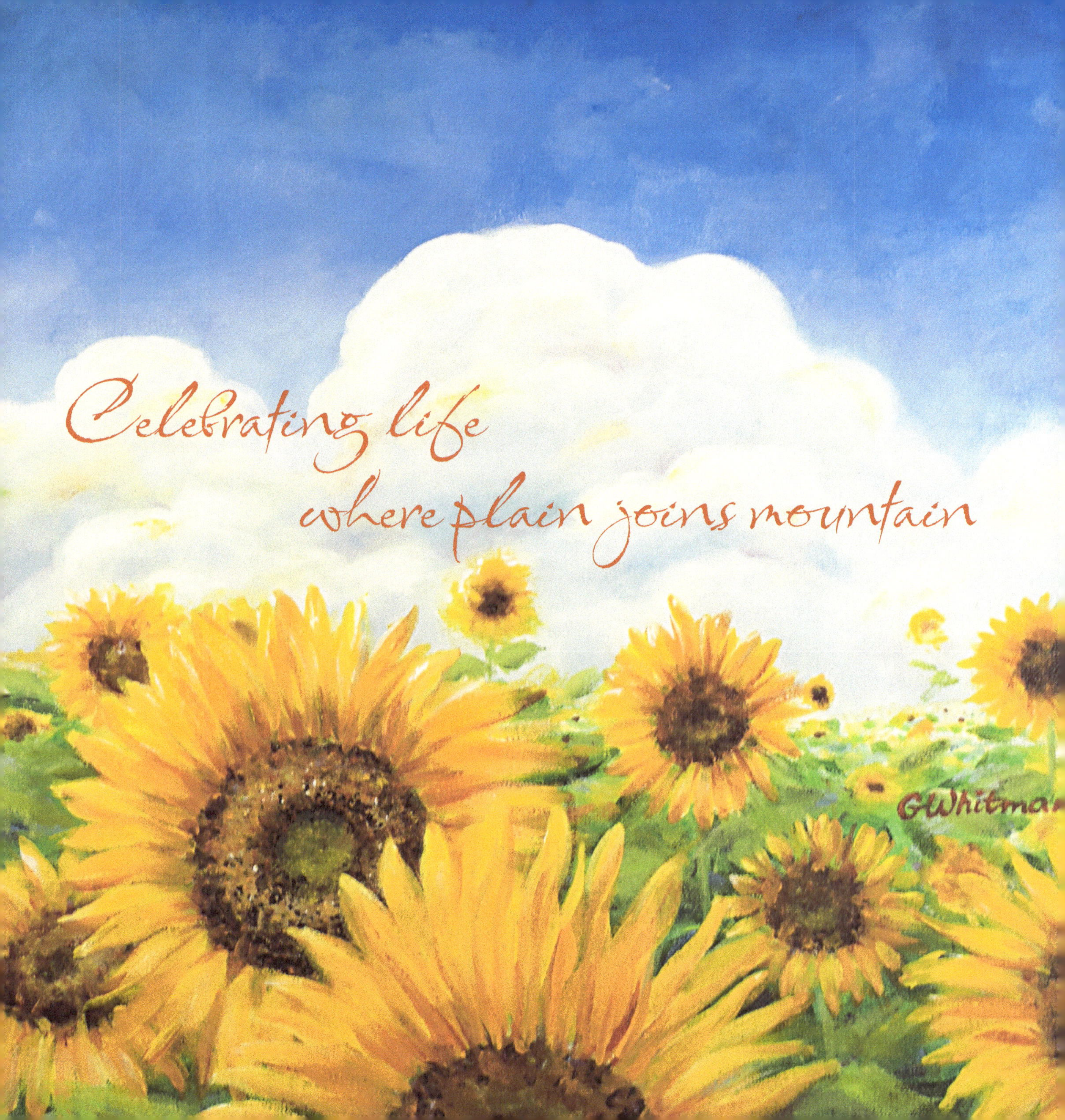
Celebrating life
where plain joins mountain
GWhitma

For the Creative Day

Yes,

we are passionate about our project.
We are passionate not because we presume
that we,
finally,
are the ones to save our imperfect species
and threatened planet,
but because it is our turn.
It is our turn
to save,
beautify,
improve,
and enjoy
our brief time and changing world.

Every generation,
each century,
each millennium
challenges our species and our planet,
because our species and planet challenge each other.
Our 21st Century is at once both unique and no different.

passion

celebrate

Abundance,
we have stolen it, produced it,
consumed it, wasted it,
leaving residue of pleasure and guilt.

Nature,
the living world of which we are but a
small part,
we threaten with crassness and calories.

Technology,
we embrace, but seldom understand it;
we connect through it while feeling more
disconnected;
we demand that it move us faster while we
dream of slowing down;
and for every fear it erases we discover
new anxiety.

Mortality,
we know more about it than our ancestors
but seem to find it harder to accept.

Yet,
every depressing hour calls out for the
creative day
that we insist on having.
Seasoned
we are by trials.
Inspired
we are by beauty,
generosity,
sensitivity,
resilience,
the creative optimism of others
that we find humbly reflected in ourselves.
In well-seasoned optimism
we acknowledge struggles,
share joys,
encourage each other—
among others.
As we marvel at how much we have
in common
we celebrate our differing skills.
In fond, artistic union
we celebrate
what we make audible
of what one sees,
and what we make visible
of what one hears.

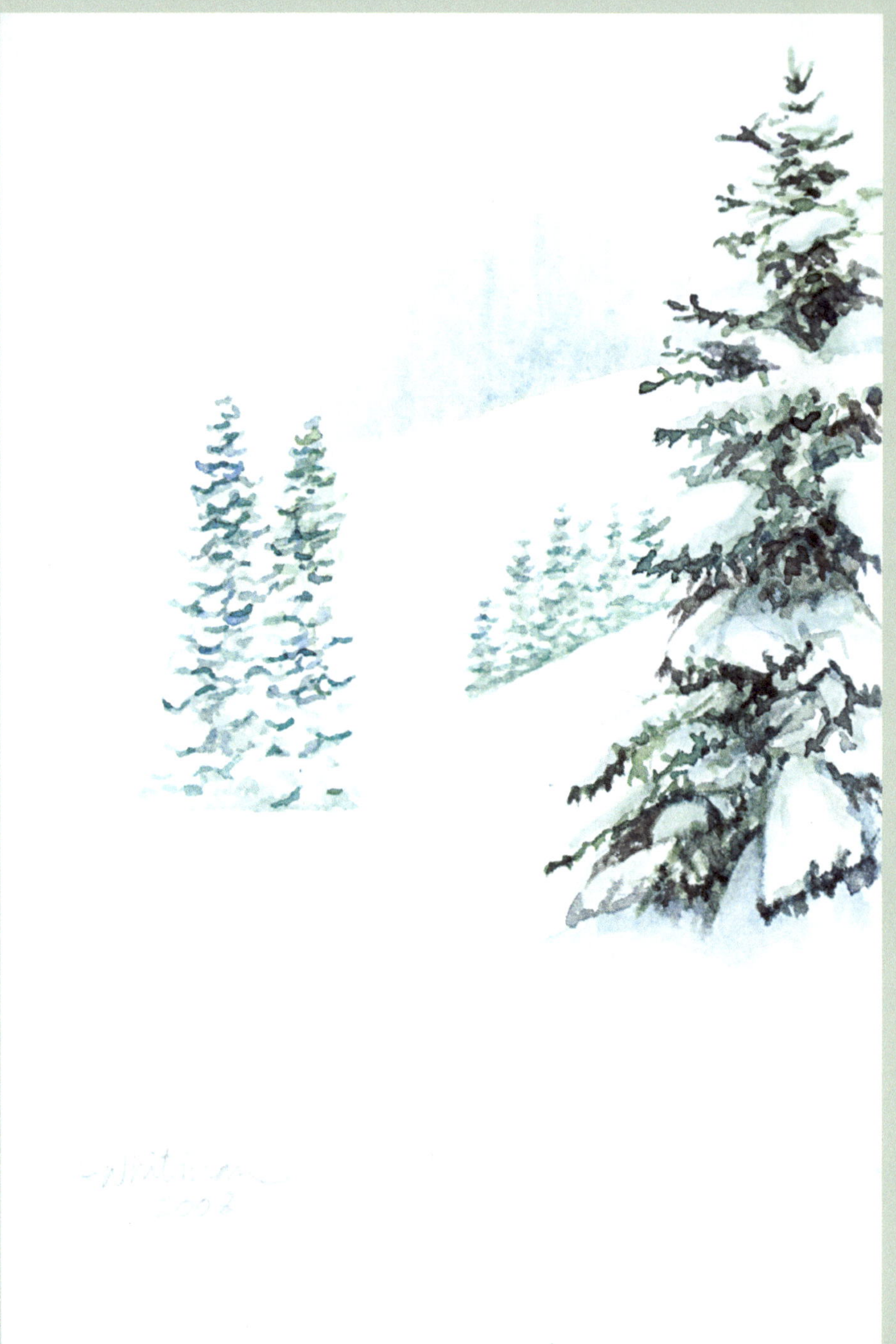

See your own breath 'round

Hear your own steps sound

Winter

With Cold Numbing Your Cheeks

With cold numbing your cheeks
and hood hiding your face,
come through the wind and door to the empty chair.

Then a view,
facing street,
heated stove,
rippled heat.
Tropical foreground.
Frozen-trunk midground.
Snow-laden branches beyond.

Through the ripples of heat
and coffee's new warmth,
record your private notes with your public stare.

Then, again,
empty seat,
wind and door,
frozen street.
See your own breath 'round.
Hear your own steps sound.
Many more errands beyond.

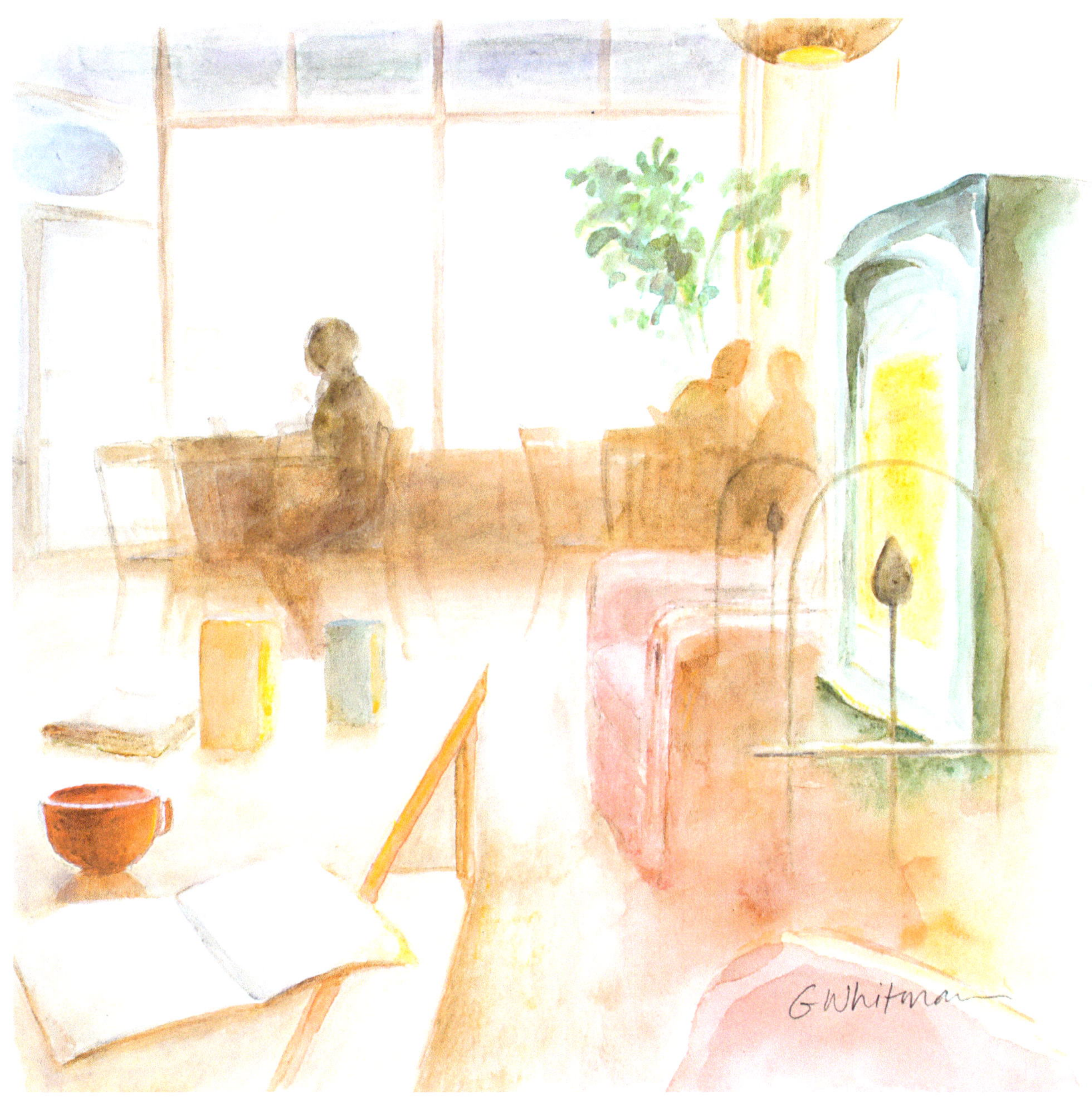

Warm Refuge

Hand-Me-Down of Hand-Me-Downs

It is privilege beyond merit
to see a hand-me-down of hand-me-downs
of shell and flesh security.

It is a hard moment
when first we reflect upon the hug we give
where always we would get one,
and then upon the hug we get
where always we would give one.
It is a hard notice
when we note what our parents no longer do
and we see our own hesitations
  become noticed.
' hard to be children of aging parents.
' hard to be parents of watching children.
' hard to be more adept,
stronger,
smarter in skills and gadgets of life
than they who were always most adept.
' hard to see our reflections in eyes of children
as they search for cracks
that might remain of gaps
that were their disadvantage in skill
  and wisdom.

Those months were precious
when acceleration by youth
preempted deceleration by age;
when we grew together,
caught up while catching up,
as child walked with parent and child
at the same speed to the same place;
when, up and down, across generations
we could give and take advice
  in equal measure,
and we could argue without threat.

Now, after short months and long years,
it is an easy moment
to reflect on the privilege in seeing this all
—a wealth in gifts not ordinary.
And extraordinary it would be
to live the opportunity
to see these gifts pass on.
For, by good fortune,
time may show what times have told:
It is privilege beyond merit
to see children of our children
watching parents
watching parents
as some of us children grow old.

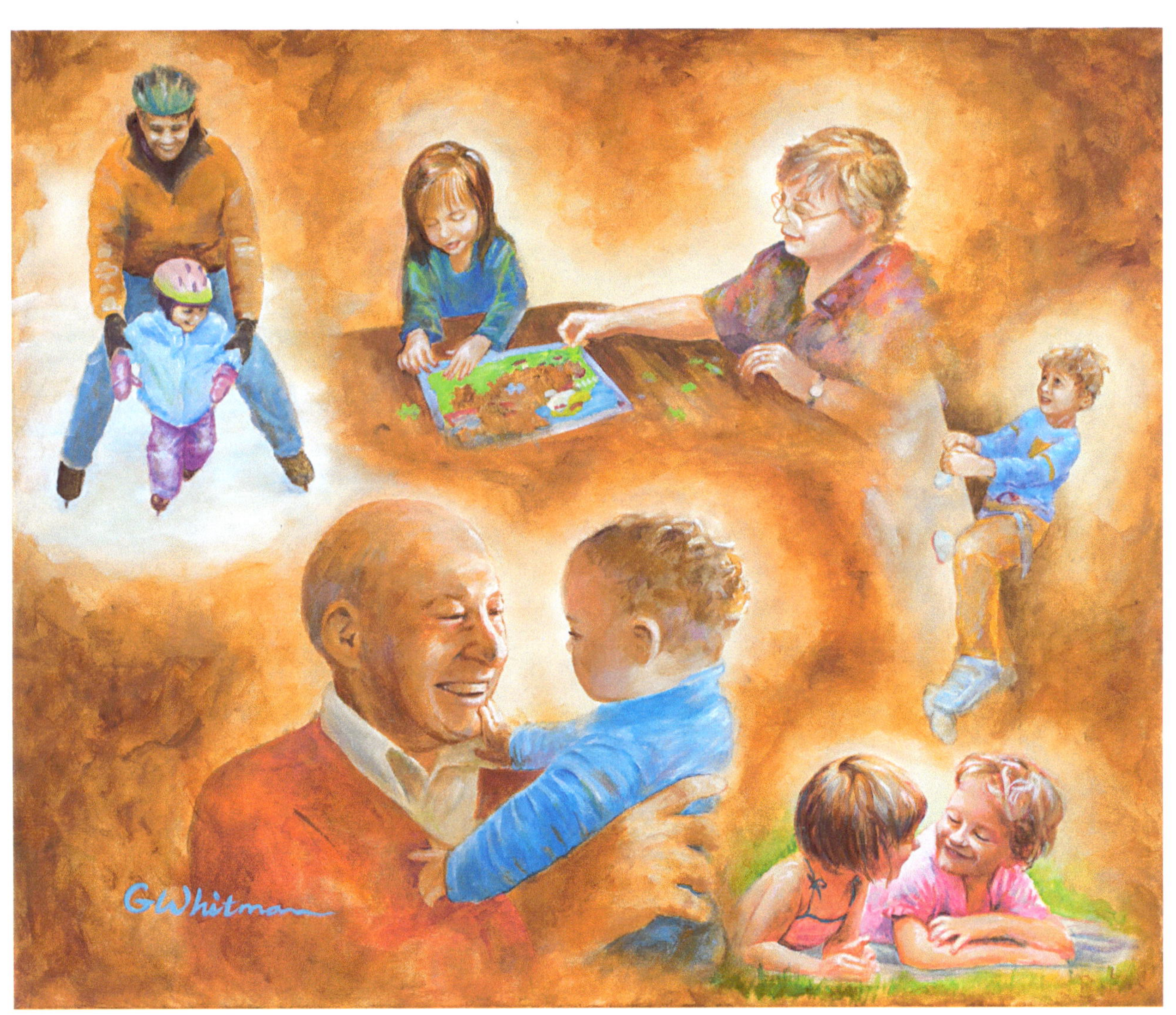

In the Hands of Time

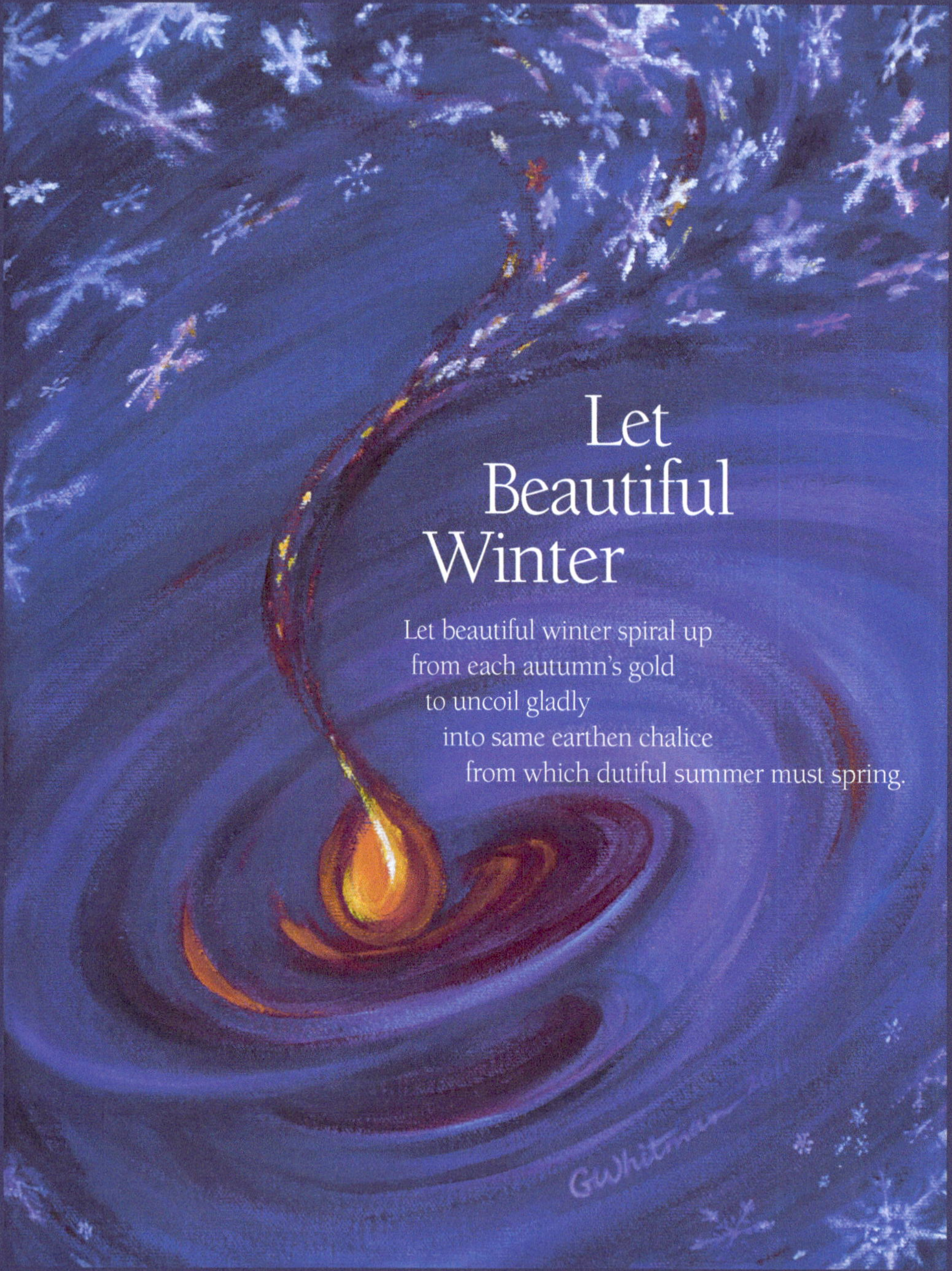

Let Beautiful Winter

Let beautiful winter spiral up
from each autumn's gold
to uncoil gladly
into same earthen chalice
from which dutiful summer must spring.

Snowlight

My Common Stove

My stove knows how to burn its firewood,
how to respond
to me who knows so little of what it knows,
to me who does not know how to make a stove.
My stove knows how to send smoke up its chimney
and warmth into my room.
Its warmth can please,
or it can save a half-frozen life.
Such is its success and popularity
that I could sell tickets to my stove's proximity.
But, I do not.
I share its warm knowledge freely
according to communal tradition
among family, neighbors, and kindred strangers.
Those whom my stove knows to please,
those whom my stove knows to save
give back nothing in trade
—except,
to carry forward in common tradition
what we and a stove
must in-common know.

Otherwise Meadow

Clump of grass
and others scattered
  strong
  dormant
  brown

Willow bush
  there
  and over there

Frozen pond beyond

Evergreen spikes and pyramids
  a few together
  and far between

Aspen family
  showing off where elk
  in winter gnaw

This rabbit track

And this song from the bird
  I cannot see

And beyond beyond
oh—yes the mountain peak
  handsome
  distant
  narcissist
  to demark earth at sky

Otherwise meadow

Everywhere meadow
  wrinkled
  humble
  artist-drop-cloth
  disguised these weeks as
    blanket of snow
  ignoring this morning those
    summer multitudes
  so that I
  I alone
  may pretend to be alone
  to own forever
  that willow there
  and this clump of grass
  dormant
  and brown

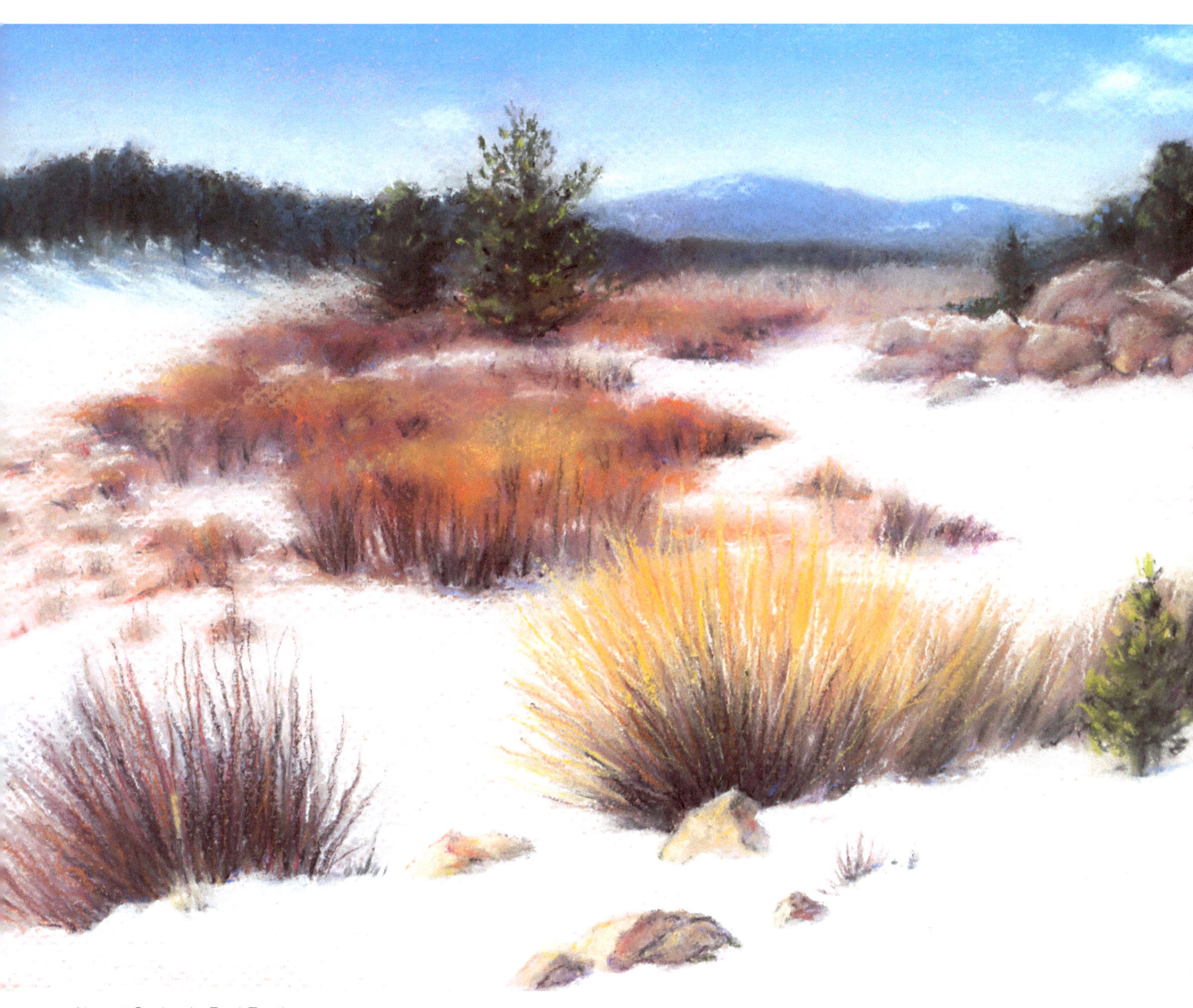

Almost Spring in Red Feather

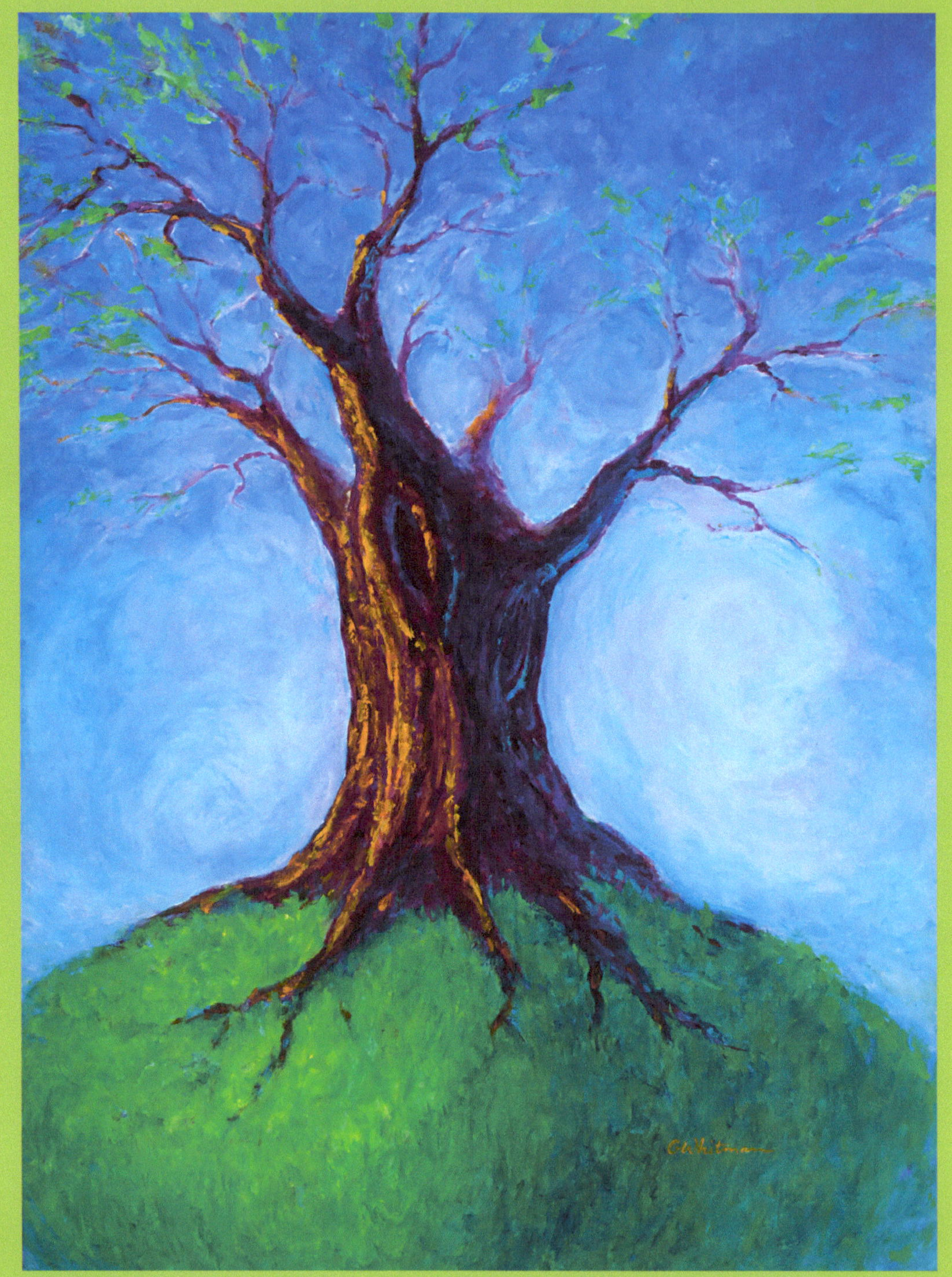
CWhitman

I wish to smell the smell,

listen to squirrels, birds, and gate

Spring

Gardens of Pleasant Regret

on prospects of returning home

I wish to see the garden,
the gardens—the tenth of an acre around my house—
    hard surfaces I laid down,
    soft earth I dug up,
    the green,
    the hues-floral,
    successes after decades of error and trial,
    the done, undone and yet to do,
    a patch of lawn that will need cutting,
    weeds that will have erupted,
    and gifts from good seeds that dropped in.
I wish to smell the smell,
listen to squirrels, birds, and gate,
and I wish to walk with pleasure and companion
as I hear—with pleasant regret—
of what I missed in the days and evenings of my absence.

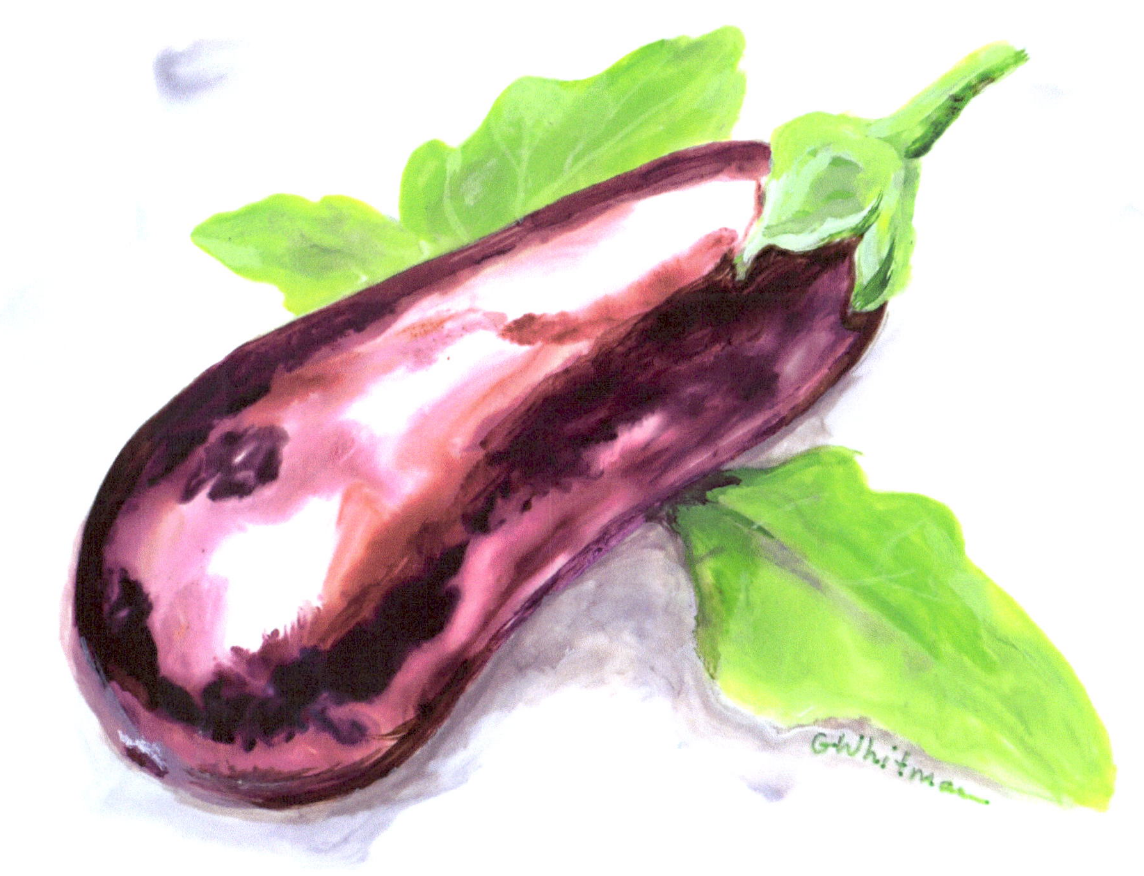

Aubergine

I Make No Note of Faces

Out the door into the sun,
I give my plants their inspection,
pull a weed,
admire a bloom,
ponder our next collaboration,
walk west
   (a few beer glasses on the lawn next door)
past the young spruce
   (thirty feet high)
that challenges my right to the sidewalk,
past two spindly green ash.
   (replacements for lost elms)
At the corner,
I do not meet the neighbor who yesterday said,
"Open that umbrella; it's not a walking stick!"
I did as I was told.
   (I was off on a long walk through the rain.)
I smile at this reflection and cross the street
enjoying the aromatic, chromatic benefits
of yesterday's twenty-hour soak.
I pass by the day-care center where kids play
and by the fraternity where they still play.
   (Though sand-filled volleyball court
      stands empty.)
Another street to cross,
I appreciate the new stripes and dashes
   (white and yellow)
that now give the street more authority over me
and over the cars and bikes that cross my path.

As I leave the curb
a white car accelerates.
   (from the traffic light one block to the north)
I jog a couple of steps,
then slow to a walk,
then stare that nuisance into deceleration.
On the far side,
I enjoy again one of the nicest houses in town,
valiantly and proudly holding its beauty
   (and its look of home)
in a block that has searched for identity
the twenty years that I have known it.
Along the wrought-iron fence
   (too low to keep in the great dane)
I wonder why the dogs stay inside.
Past another blue spruce and across an alley
I approach the avenue.
At the corner on my right
is a once-gas-station adult bookstore.
   (well-kept)
To my left,
is a once-mom-and-pop once-pizza
      now-pawn shop.
   (well-kept, but kept ugly)

to notice

Now I confront the barrier that
        divides east from west.
Beyond lies a square mile of university.
It is nine-thirty.
With no pause
    (by me nor by the traffic)
I cross four lanes and set my own path
across the broad, damp lawn on the other side.
No students toss frisbees this morning.
Few cars sit in the parking lot
that sits in my way
and sits where Old Main once stood.
    (where rumors linger as to how it burned)
Up and over
    (a not so "crooked stile")
I cross the Burlington Northern track.
    (no train in sight)
Into the old heart of campus
I skirt one quadrant
of the grass-filled, tree-lined oval
past several pieces in a set of buildings
that await recognition,
        preservation and maintenance.
    (an historic district)

The buildings sit on land
that one hundred and fifty years ago
had not sprouted its first crop of wheat.
Here,
my walk joins the walks of others.
They do not quite hurry
        to where they choose to go.
Perhaps they too feel
    (after four weeks of rain)
that it is more important to notice than to hurry.
    (Noticing does slow us down.)
We hurried out this morning.
    (into the sun)
We'll be damned if we'll now hurry in.
I note this rhythm.
    (strange, but)
I make no note of faces.
This is a day for smells and for colors.
    (And this is a day for spaces.)

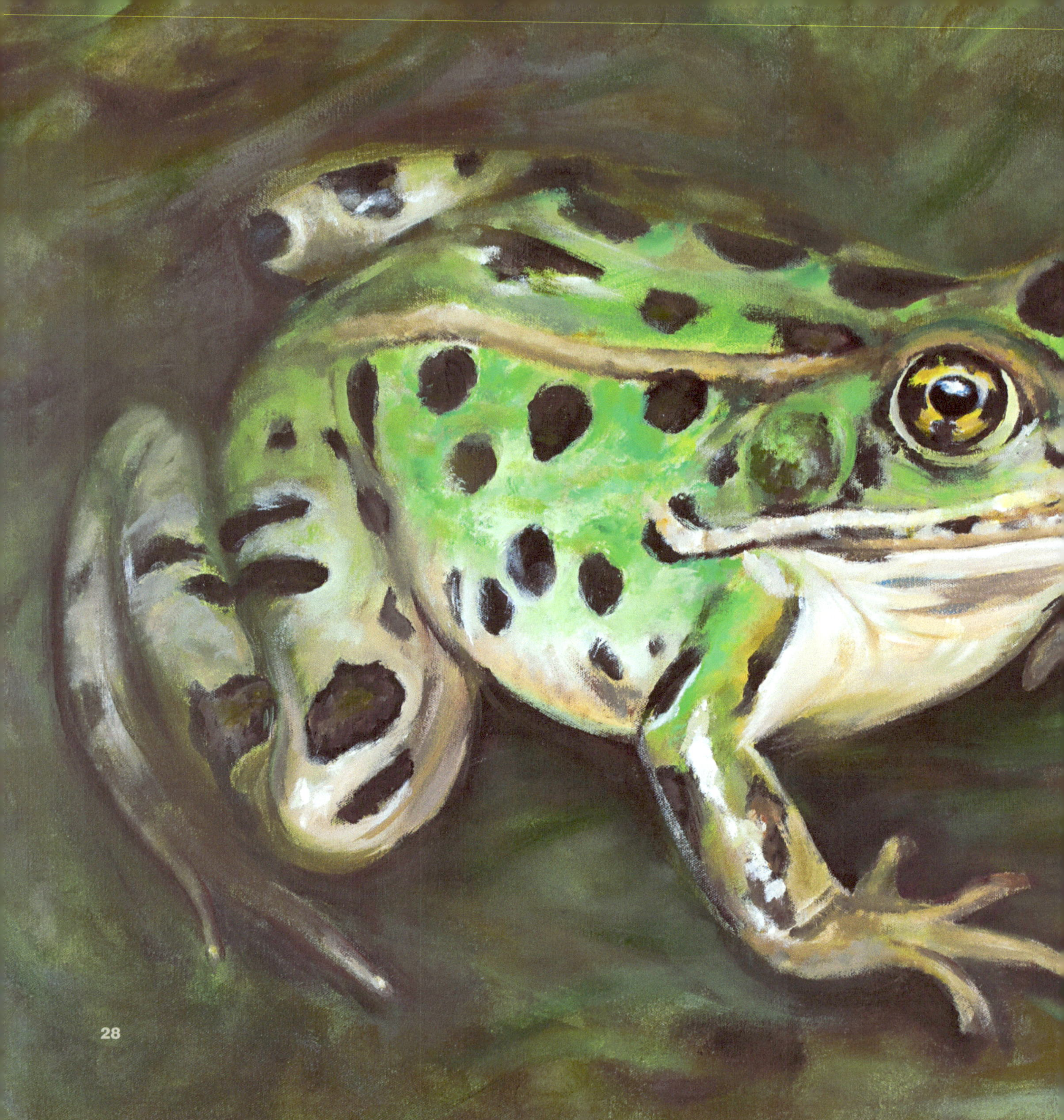

I am Fibian

I am Fibian,
northern leopard frog.
This place is one of my spots.
I was once so common
along Cache La Poudre River,
up and down
across North America,
you did not count me for much.
But such is history.
Today,
you do not count me for many.
I am Fibian,
cold-blooded amphibian.
Relative to many of my relatives
I am fine
(though in precipitous decline)
because still you can find me.
That is hard to say of my cousin,
Boreal Toad,
supposed to live near the mountain
headwater.
He is obviously and officially
endangered,
while I am just Fibian,
northern leopard frog,
another amphibian
in the official state of special concern.
I am three and one half inches long.
I take well to cold
but do not freeze.

I eat insects
and other things that would upset
your stomach.
Some of you say I am spotted green
to be spotted in the meadow during
summer vacation.
Some of you say I am spotted
brown to be spotted in deep
water, pond, and wetland.
I crisscross your roads in
spring and fall
to prove that none of you
is wrong.
But something is wrong
along the river,
around the world.
I am Fibian,
frog, amphibian;
listen up!
When I croak you jump!
In wetland mud I draw a line.
Hop to it and heed my sign:
Beyond this point
river stays open
to song and dance and
occasional rhyme,
but valley is closed
to amphibian decline.

Fibian

I Live Where Strangers Smile

I live where strangers smile—
where we acquire kinship-by-encounter
on common paths with crossing points—
where the names we seem to have forgotten
are those we have yet to learn.
Rather than meet
up-and-down
ear-by-ear
by elevator,
we meet
face-to-face
on ramp and stair.
Our doorholding
gets traded among old and young—
so we need not know which we are.
Our "thank you"
(if warranted)
gets given.
Our information
(if needed)
gets exchanged.
Our frivolous word or friendly observation
(if it might fit)
might get fitted.
I live in a place with public smiles for private eyes
on common paths with crossing points.
If you know such place,
perhaps you too know me.

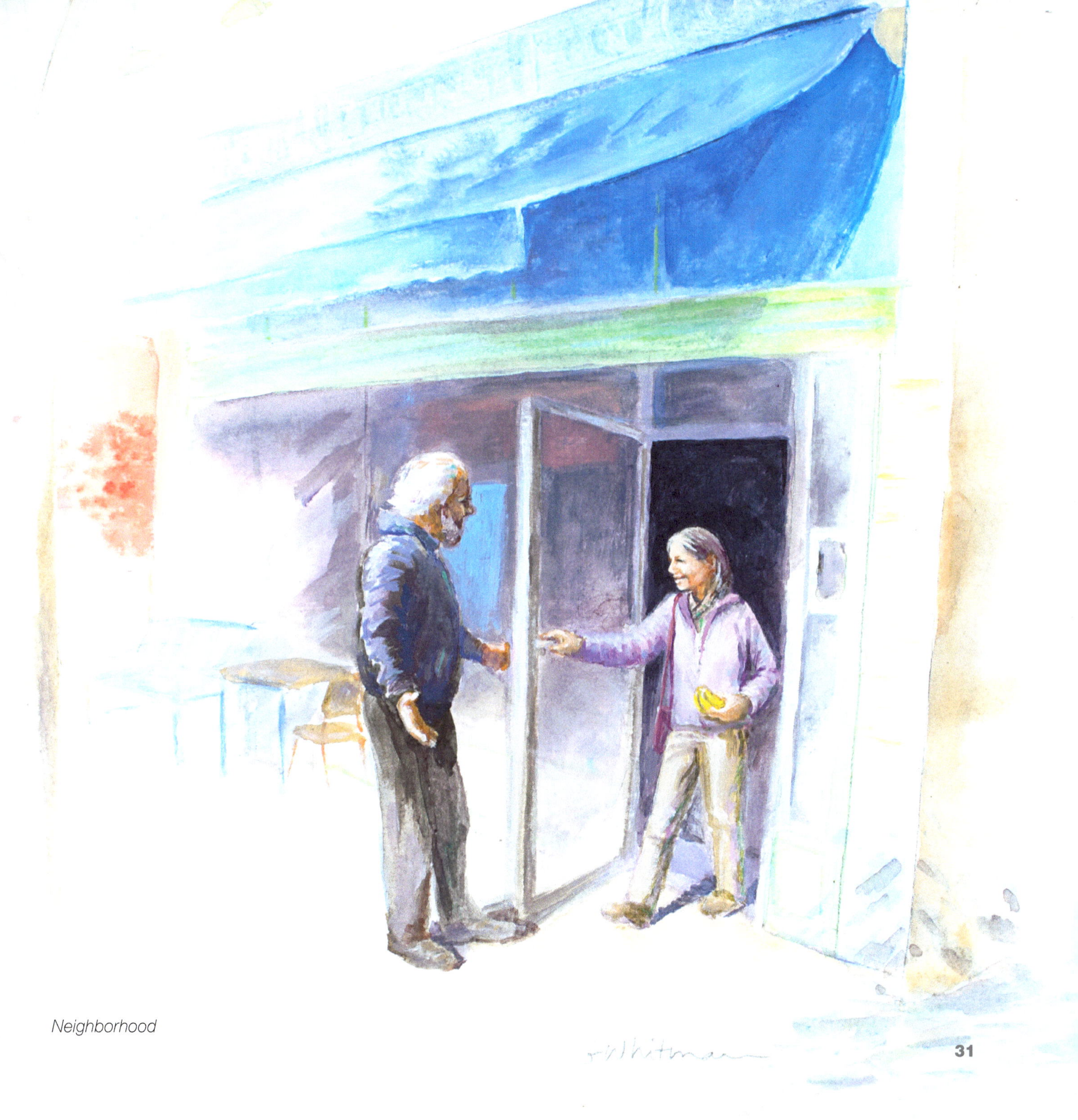

Neighborhood

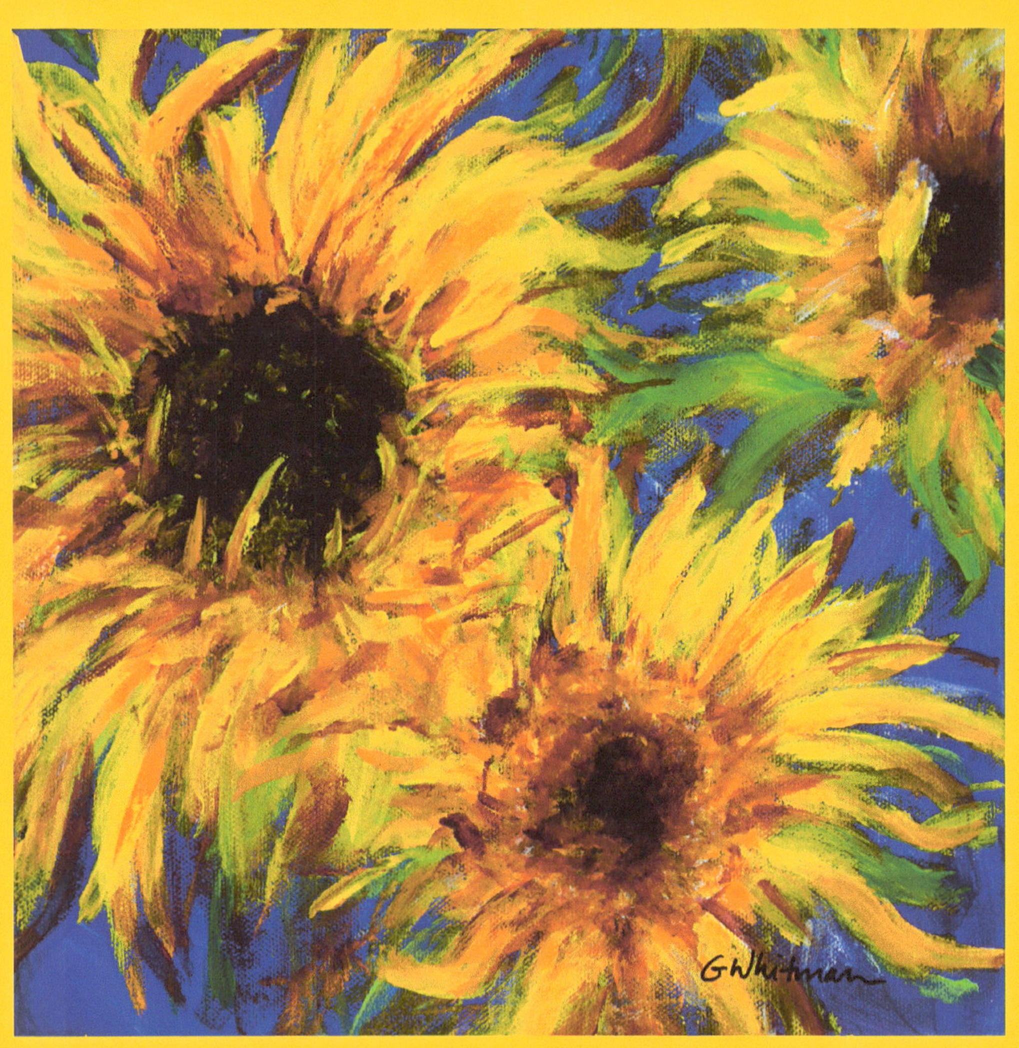

if we share two places,

we will meet for the first time as old friends.

Summer

Turn to Sun

This early morning
he passes from Mississippi headwater
out of woodland and wetland
across the Red River onto North Dakota
—rolling plain of North Dakota—
a perfect expanse (said Buckminster Fuller)
a perfect expanse on which to feel oneself
spin toward the sun at early light
and spin away at late light.
He likes that it bothered Fuller
when people speak "sunrise"
—for the sun does not rise—
and "sunset"
—for the sun does not set.
It is we on our planet who spin from the sun:
turn from the sun each evening
turn to the sun each morning.
Today,
he has convinced himself; he does sense it
just as Fuller said he would.
He drives on, smug with satisfaction,
hypnotized, rolling northeast to southwest.

until
he startles from his meditation.
They are looking at him—
bronze little faces
fringed in yellow bonnet-and-bib.
Sunflowers by the thousands, millions,
sunflowers looking at him.

He ignores the obvious truth:
they look to the sun behind him.
To be twice smug he puts his Spanish vocabulary
to work:
"girasol" "turn to sun"
Indeed, better words
for both "sunrise" and "sunflower."
Installed in his driver's seat,
he is philosopher royal to the northern great plain.
Throngs of sunflowers
crowd in for his morning audience.
Narcissistic pleasure.

until
he startles from his meditation.
They will not look at him beyond morning.
(He cannot drive faster than earth spins)

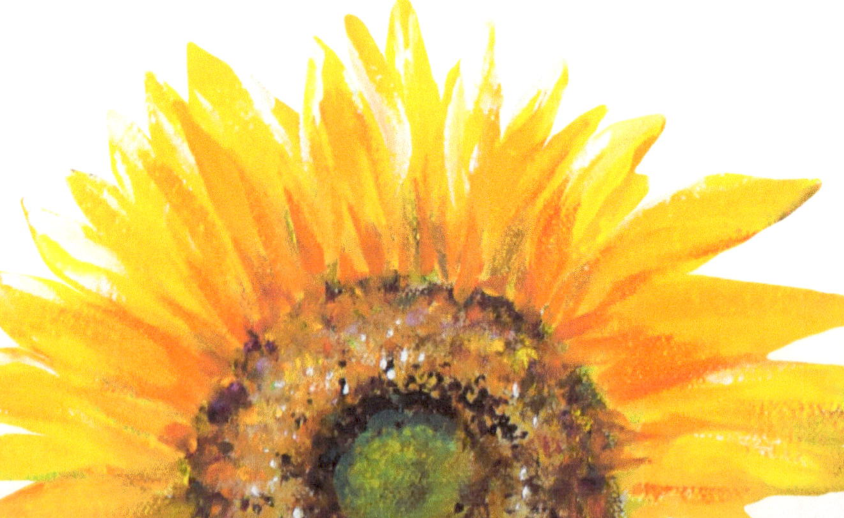

Good Day

So as not to be dethroned,
he abdicates to take more pleasure
in the seeing than the being seen.
Find a sunflower at each road bend—
one among the many,
one to appreciate for her skill and beauty.
"Good Day," nods he,
"Good Day," nods she,
For, indeed, it is!

Now west, then south; west and south again,
toward where young waters flow
onto a place among many
where old plain both begins and ends.
Now, on minor highway,
through well-kept town,
past well-kept cemetery,
(too large for its few occupants)
past silo and farm,
through deep carpet of sunflowers
and his chosen beauties.

Each earns—as true beauty earns—
his lingering gaze
as a breeze inspires her sensual sway.

until,
for one,
he slows, pulls over, stops,
lingers in flirtation.
Now more golden than yellow,
she offers her profile.
He hears words,
but which of them whispered?
"Good day,
smug friend,
Good day."
For, indeed, it is!

Sun on Their Faces (detail)

Will Archeologist Dig Us Up?

We inter kitchen waste in our garden where it
helps us produce
tomatoes,
lettuce,
and beans,

which, in turn, make garden debris and
kitchen waste for us to bury where they will
help us produce
tomatoes,
lettuce,
and beans.

With burning banned and land fill filling, we should match production to our rate of decay. We do not. Our garden rises. Every fifth year we add three and one-half inches of timber around rising vegetables in our risen soil. Elsewhere in our yard the rise is subtle. Our house sinks without moving. Patio and walk descend to become pond and river, while culprit flowers and lawn look innocent.

I never understood why archaeologist must unearth cities, dig down, and further down through past city below, into lost civilization beneath, to disinter them, bring them up and out, from oblivion into history. I did not understand until I noticed my land grow upward at millennial pace toward burial of my home—obscuring:
noble purpose,
romance,
our sense of good citizenship
in burial of garbage
where
and when
we live.

Our commandments are noble and moral,
are they not?
Live with our garbage!
Make it useful!
And, in turn,
Fight erosion!
Erosion robs soil and nutrient—carries them away as spoil and pollution. I do seek to prevent erosion—have supported its prevention by others. Lately, however, as I inter bucketfuls of kitchen waste I unearth questions:
Will archaeologist dig us up?
with purpose?
by accident?
How tiny is that likelihood?
for this era?
my neighborhood?
Or, is erosion the only likely future,
humble accident,
ignoble story
that may keep us above oblivion?

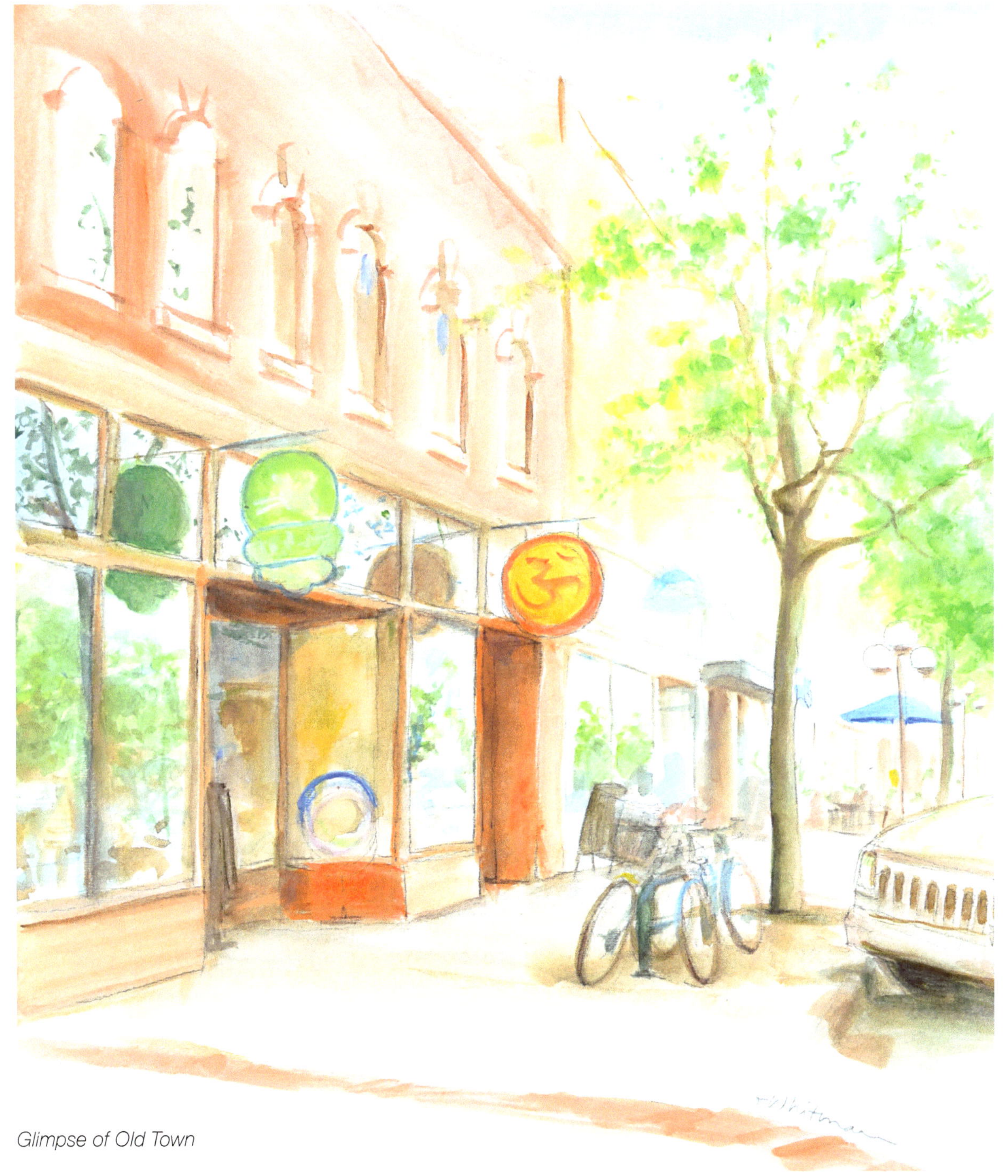

Glimpse of Old Town

Shadow of Our Photographer

How many people have come here
once in one lifetime?
    from other continents and this,
    from down the road a bit,
    during summer of 39 or Autumn of 93,
    before or after,
    to look at this mountain and that valley,
    to walk a few steps on this trail,
    to take this photograph
    that sits in how many albums
    showing familiar figures
    who stand before known stone and tundra,
    and showing unknown figures
    who take the same picture.

I have come thirty times.
First, from a thousand miles and forty years away.
Now, through twenty years from forty miles.
Each time I stand in awe
of this public beauty and my private privilege,
and, for a moment,
each time I imagine all who have shared them.

Sometimes,
far from here,
among strangers
enjoying separately a common experience,
I think of here
and want to ask if we have it in common too
—a memory that would make us kin.

I have never braved that question.
But, here, today,
I will ask you about a distant place I once visited.
For if we share two places
we will meet for the first time as old friends.

No matter your answer,
we will go separate ways
to add like photograph to like album,
to write, perhaps,
a note about this place,
and include, perhaps,
something about the shadow of our
photographer.

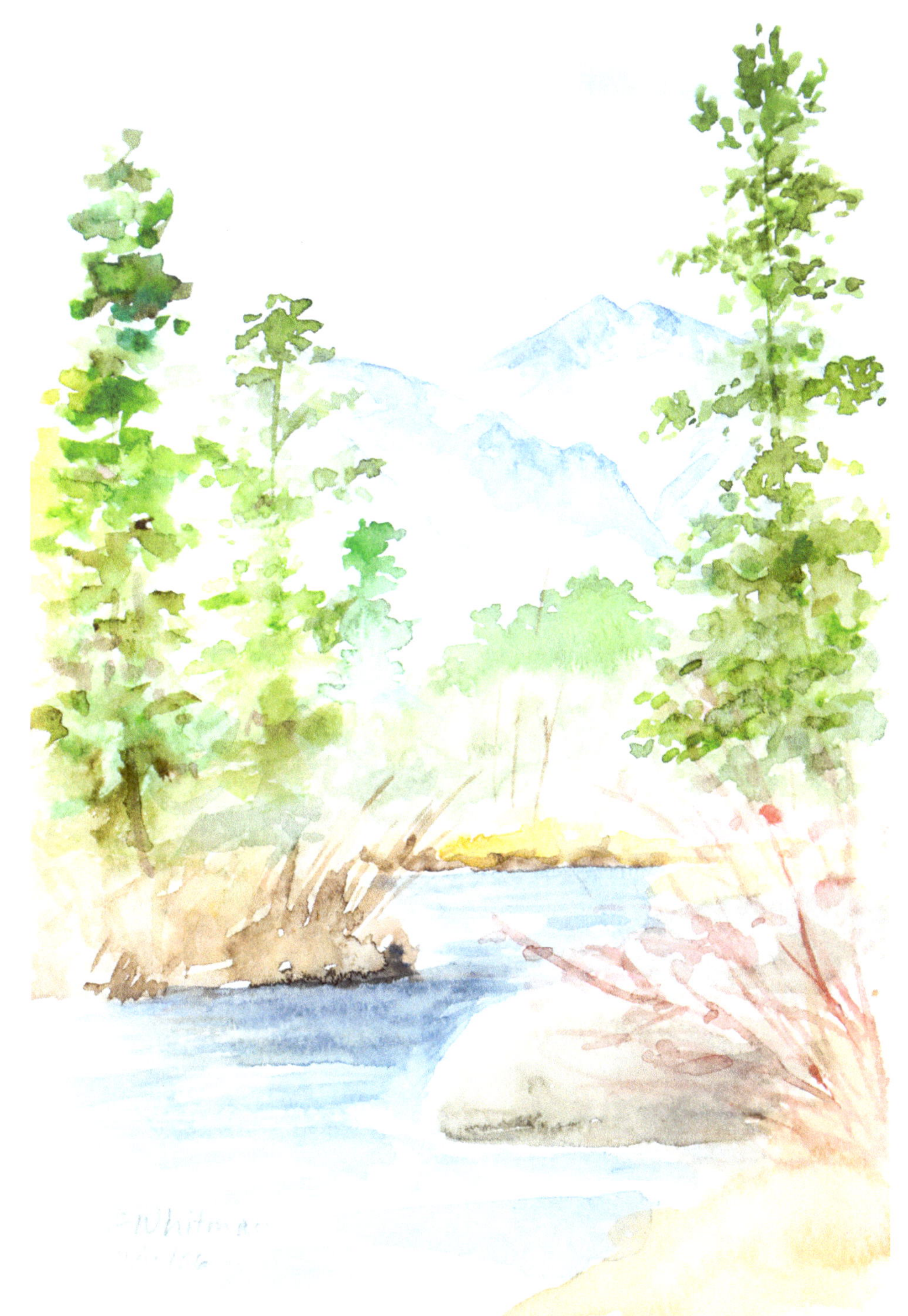

Postcard to
My Children

Good Day, Passers-by

Good day, Passer-by,
I watch you pass.
I am pleased when you stop.

You see us all around
as you build your city on our ground.
Perhaps because we do not flee
you think us to be thriving.
But we have lost
ninety-nine percent of our land,
ninety-nine percent of our home ground,
the great North American Prairie
where we build and maintain our towns,
where we built cities
before your species came around.
If we look proud,
we are proud.
Wherever Buffalo roamed we built homes.
We made the great prairie what it was
and can be.
We till the land,
propagate grasses,
release our homes to burrowing owls,
insects,
snakes,
countless species
who do not know how to make a home
unless first we develop the land.
We install utility,
maintain ability
of prairie to be prairie.

Good day, Passer-by.
I am pleased when you stop.
I am Prairie Dog,
a rodent with complex language,
sophisticated society,
commitment to family.
I am your good neighbor.
I know to live with you.
Can you learn and live with me?

I do not care for the eagle,
nor the hawk,
ferret,
coyote,
fox,
nor wolf.
They have taken away family
and want to prey upon me.
Yet I have learned to live with them.
They depend on me.
I am great prairie's great friend.
If you are fond of eagle,
remember me;
I am your great eagle's greater friend.

I am prairie citizen.
On the last one percent of my homeland
I can live with you.
The prairie is passing, Fellow Citizen.
It will slow as you stop,
and it will grow when you show
you can live with me.

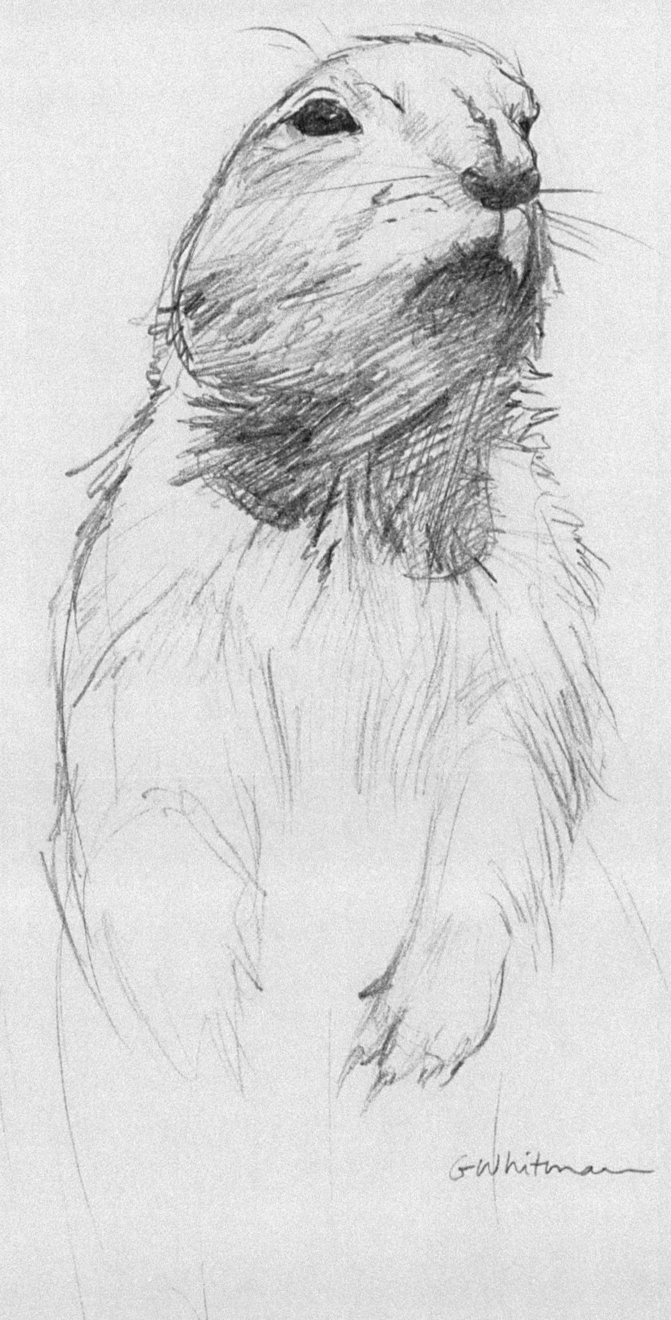

Watchdog

The Bicycle

an ode to fun

The bicycle is a kind machine.
It will take you up any road up any hill,
if, indeed, your muscle will.

Then coming down, with your muscle toned,
your bicycle will do it all alone.

Yes, it will—
while you sit still.

Yes, it will.

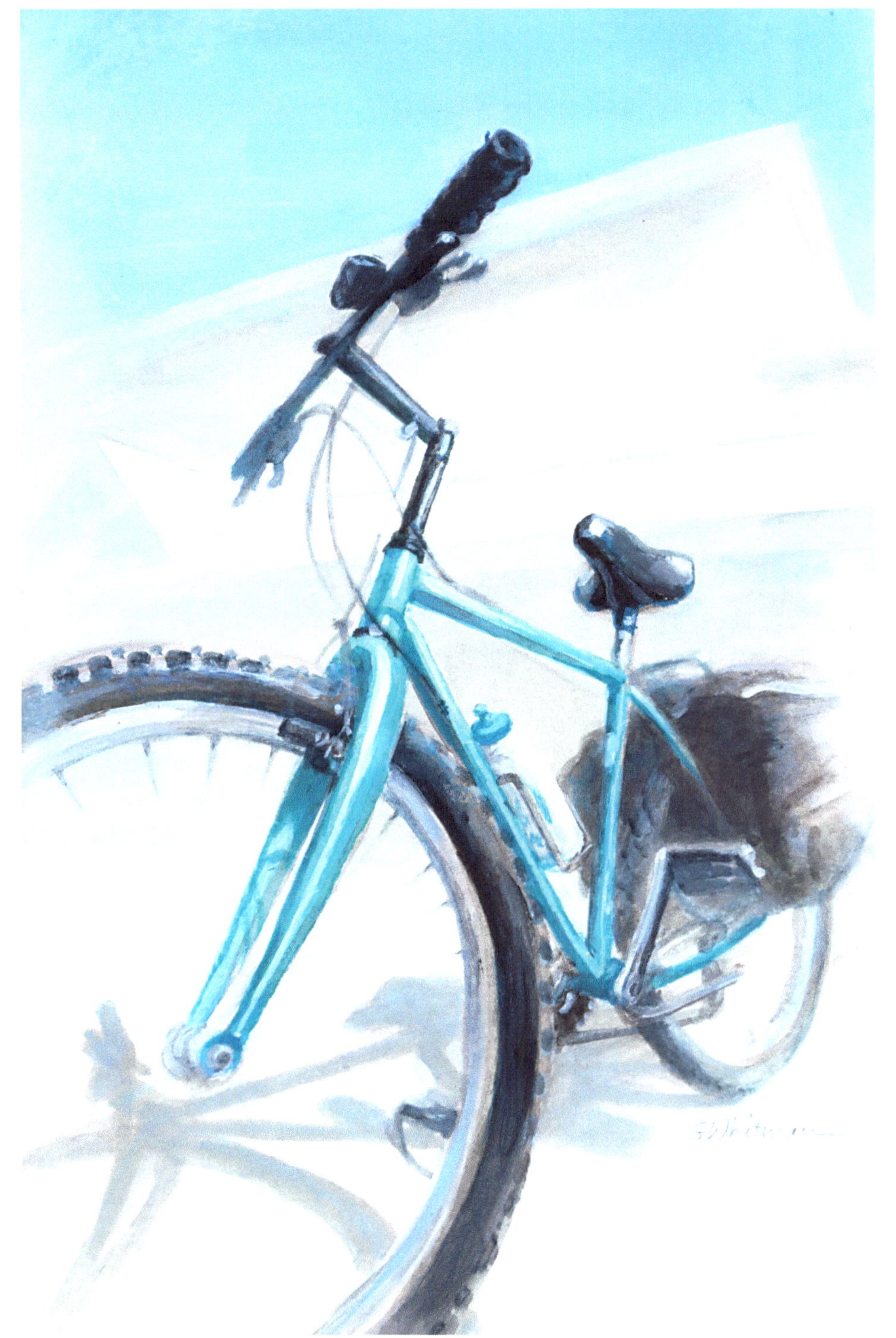

My Trusty Steed

Fortuitous Stop in McCook

We drive east
on western high plain,
through hill-full prairie,
under afternoon sun,
into the Nebraska town of McCook.

Room secured to pass the night
we drive downtown to look around
and naively notice:
        here too is history.
The station waits
for zephyr-train to stop and pass,
but not as proudly as four decades past
when one of us rolled in at night
on the move to California.
We drive past nurtured relics
of shop and office and banking past.
Up the hill
past elegant homes from oil's boom past
we pass the home of a native son,
famous in high-plains history.
We congratulate ourselves for the fortuitous stop
and condemn ourselves for the snobs we must be
to be surprised
to be pleased
with an hour's exploration of McCook.
Yet, this past good hour
is humble preface to a better moment.

Discovery

As we start down hill to look for a meal
we glance
from park on our left
to corner on our right
into an instant of recognition.
We slow to pause
for our breath of surprise
and smile of discovery.
On this corner stands a house,
a family's home,
marked by no sign,
but too obvious to mistake.
Conceived before us,
modern beyond us,
it is beautiful witness to genius past.

As a woman exits the front door,
picks up a hose
and waters the lawn,
we agree that we see
behind the spray,
in front of the sunset,
a great architect returning our smile
as if he both acknowledges our appreciation
and makes arrogant claim to life after death.

As we drive on,
we nod our approval.
For, here at somebody's home
on a corner in McCook,
here above the plain in Nebraska
where we happen to pass the night,
here still lives the architect
at the house of Frank Lloyd Wright.

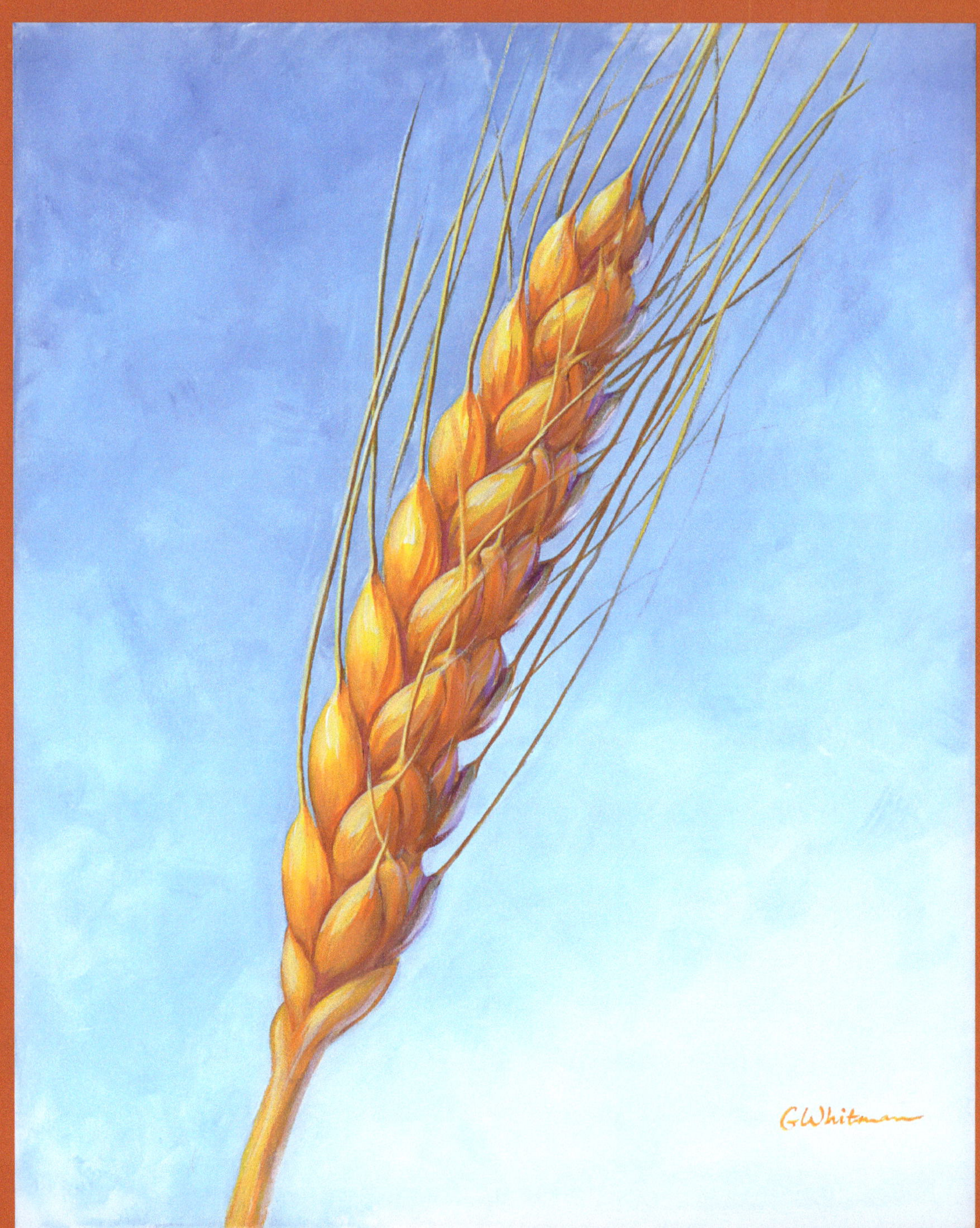
GWhitman

Let there be one cold soak
to finish one good book
and to give the earth more smell

Autumn

My Weather

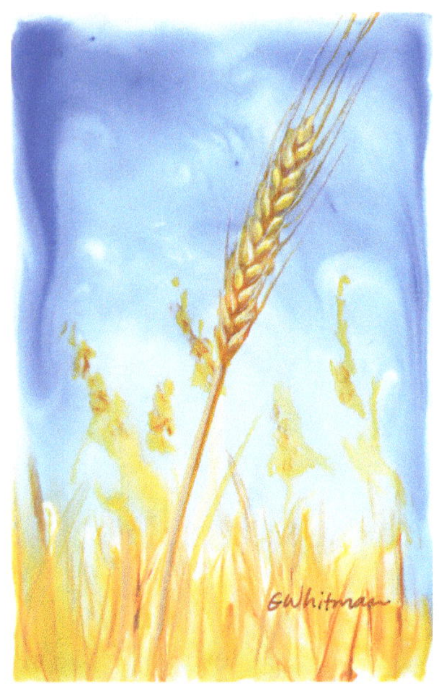

In the spring,
farmer and I
conflict over rain,
as do I
with the me
in my garden.

Not in Fall.
Good wine weather
is my weather.
Good apple picking
is my weather.
Grain-harvest time
that's my weather.

Clean the garden;
walk the morning,
sun and dry.
Do more thinking;
walk the evening,
cool and dry.

Let there be one cold soak
to finish one good book
and to give the earth more smell.

Then let sun
bring back air
crisp in shadows,
warm in light,
moving by day,
calm by night.

That's my weather.

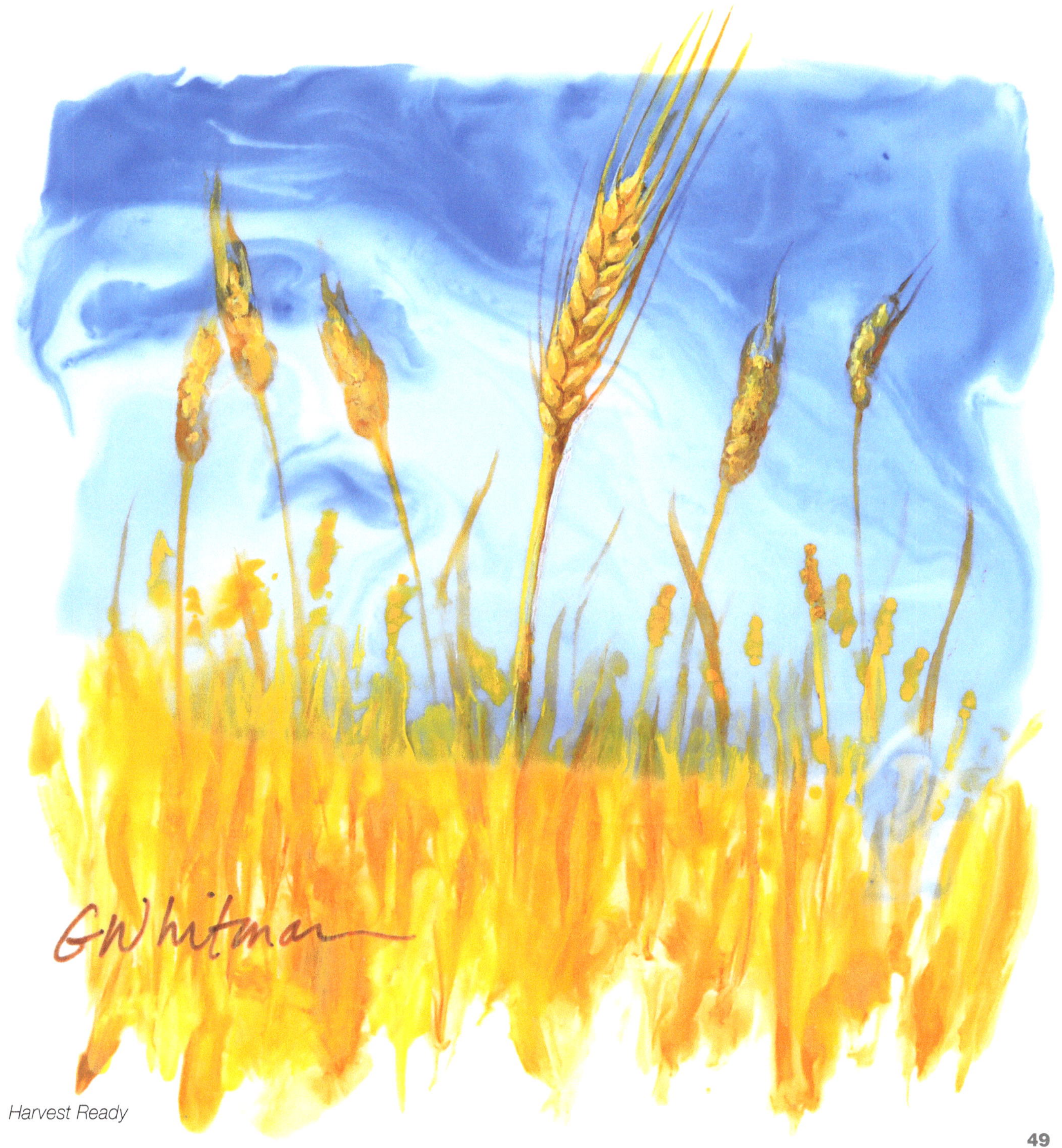

Harvest Ready

Two Men Chanced Together in Their Flight

Chanced together were this one man
and the birdman,
touching shoulders, going southward on a flight.
There this one man told the birdman his long story,
seeking confirmation that in truth what happened
is what he saw.
So the birdman, as a birdman, had to hear him:
about sitting, about back porch, and a cat;
about noises from some watchbirds
on the phone line,
perching up there watching, perching there together,
though not alike;
one, two species, three birds set to watching;
sleepy cat yawns followed by alarms;
silence, a stretch, and then a warning.
Was this one man truly hearing what he saw?
Catlike sleeping, birdlike silence, watchlike vigil.
Six eyes watching, then two species worth of noise.
Every cat move duly sounded —for no reason
until distant action, the distant reaction,
caught this man's eye.
In far corner of the yard he saw them feeding;
four, five species, forty birds there picking food.
Then the cat stretch got reported
from the phone line.
(Still this man was doubting that
in truth what happened
is what he saw.)
Four, five species, each bird was reacting,
head up, eyes up, springing to alert.
Some would fly back into the bushes;
all stopped eating; some retreated to the fence.

When the cat showed no more movement
but his sleeping,
the three lookouts were but looking down again,
and the back flock had returned again
to feeding.
(Still this man was doubting that
in truth what happened
is what he saw.)

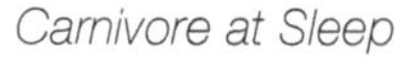

Carnivore at Sleep

Other stretching, other warning, then reaction.
Four, five species somehow acting like one flock.
Forty-bird incorporation lacking likeness.
In some common language,
        to some common purpose,
    by common mind,
different feathers, odd birds, flocked together.
Not a family, yet having that sound.
Not a platoon, yet having sergeants.
Nothing studied had prepared him for these facts.

Then a cat yawn stretched to rising up and forward,
up and slowly (with eyes open) down a step.
With the rising came the warning called out louder
—the distant reaction readily upgraded
    to high alert.
As the cat stepped (with eyes searching)
        to the walkway,
as the watchbirds crackling louder took to flight,
back yard feeders flew from ground
        and flew from bushes
over the back fences to the safer tree limbs
    beyond the yard.
By the time the old cat got to walking,
nowhere back there would there be a bird,
nowhere platoon, nor crackling sergeant.
Nor could this man show another what he saw.

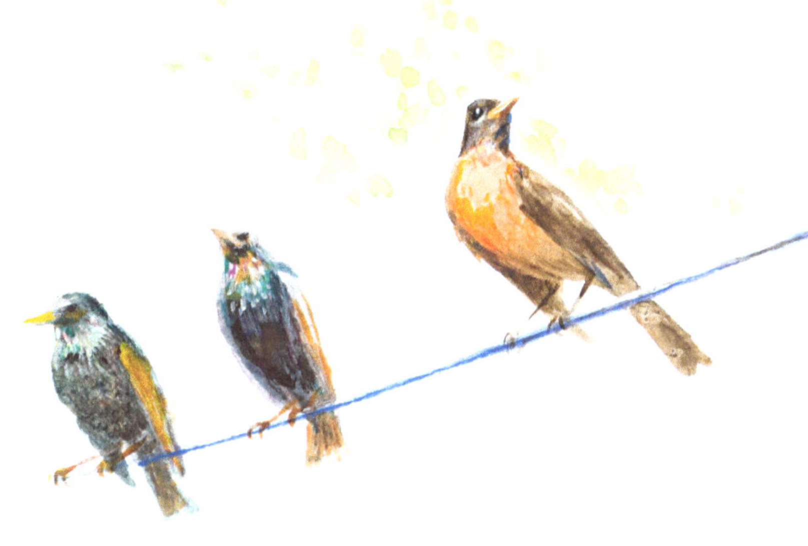

Then the birdman (who had listened)
        did the speaking.
In his life-long search he had seen but only three.
You did witness then a mix-of-species flocking.
Several individuals, several different species
    that work as one
come together as late Summer turns to Autumn
—for their feeding, for protection, perhaps fun.
Having bonded, no new members can then enter.
Every individual is exclusive member
    within this flock
—until leaving by types for their winters.
It's a privilege for anyone to see.
Silence, two yawns of satisfaction.
One, two birdmen chanced together in their flight.

November Five: Below the Ankles

November Five.
Alive in a long, warm autumn.
A walk across the college campus.
Feelings of being over-dressed and over-aged.
A day to look around.

Who wears his cap bill-back?
Of which tribe are he and she and they?
Who wears her cap bill-front?
Of which tribe are she and they and he?
Can I trust conclusions from years of observation?
The Bill-fronts have come back
(from near extinction)
to dominate.
Have they prospered by conversion?
in-migration?
propagation?
war?
No matter the explanation,
a more obvious observation:
  the hat on my head is popular
  only among dermatologists.
Conveniently too warm,
I stow hat into pocket
and join the inconspicuous tribe
(yet populous tribe)
of No-bills.
This humble act pulls my eyes down
to where I happen to notice feet,
two, three pairs of feet,
walking and standing
(to my surprise)
on the thonged sandals I know as flip flops.
Surpised,
pleased,
these artifacts too avoid extinction
after tenuous years of survival
inside a few shower rooms,
outside on lonely July beaches,
and, of course,
here on a warm November day
on my two feet.
They survived verbal abuse
from cross-foot-sandal tribes,
from friend and family.
During its ascendance
the cross-foot became more rugged,
more varied,
expensive—
kicking humble flip flops from the landscape.
But today I see three,
four, five young women of fashion
wearing sturdy, expensive flip flops.
They signal a re-born trend,
and acknowledge me as leader.

I walk off campus,
more alive,
newly aligned,
and rejuvenated below the ankles.

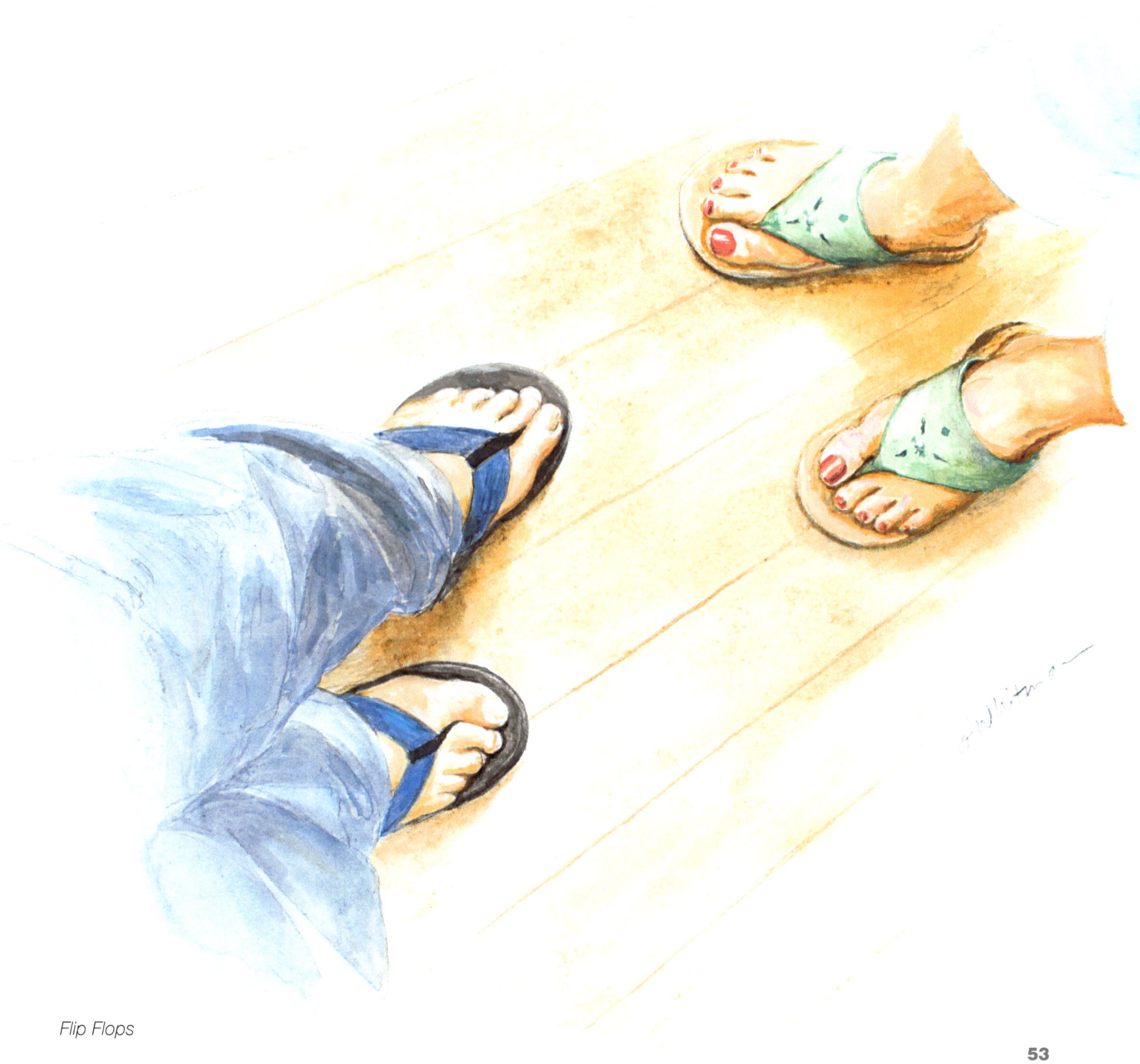

Flip Flops

Leaf on My Floor

You, leaf on my floor,
inside my house,
in through my door,
you, done with your work,
unwanted leaf,
get out!
out to my fire to burn!

I, boot on your stem,
bend,
blood to my head,
stop,
kink to my back,
feel,
guilt to my heart,
smile,
time to rethink.

You, leaf on my floor,
found under foot,
blown through the door:
I know
generations of your ancestors
helped my tree
make energy from sun,
grow,
give out seeds
and give me beauty;
I know
this year's beauty included you.

I, months ago,
    said to a friend,
    look at the beauty in that tree
    leafing out.
Weeks ago,
    I said, look!
    look at the beauty in that tree
    turning red.
Hours ago,
    I said, look outside!
    as leaves fell beautifully
    in autumn wind.
Now,
    some class of hypocrite am I
    to treat a leaf on my floor
    as clod of waste
    to put out the door.

If this were a just world
I would be found guilty of leaf
  slaughter
or reckless abandonment,
imprisoned in a cell
where I could see no leaf,
no tree,
no change of season;
in a cell so clean
it could never know you
nor twig,
nor seed,
nor speck of fertile mud.

I, blood into my heart,
guilt out through my head,
pride straight up my back,
say, come now,
dear Leaf,
dear Retired Leaf.
I take you up from my floor,
back through my door,
to beneath our tree
and set you gently to rest.

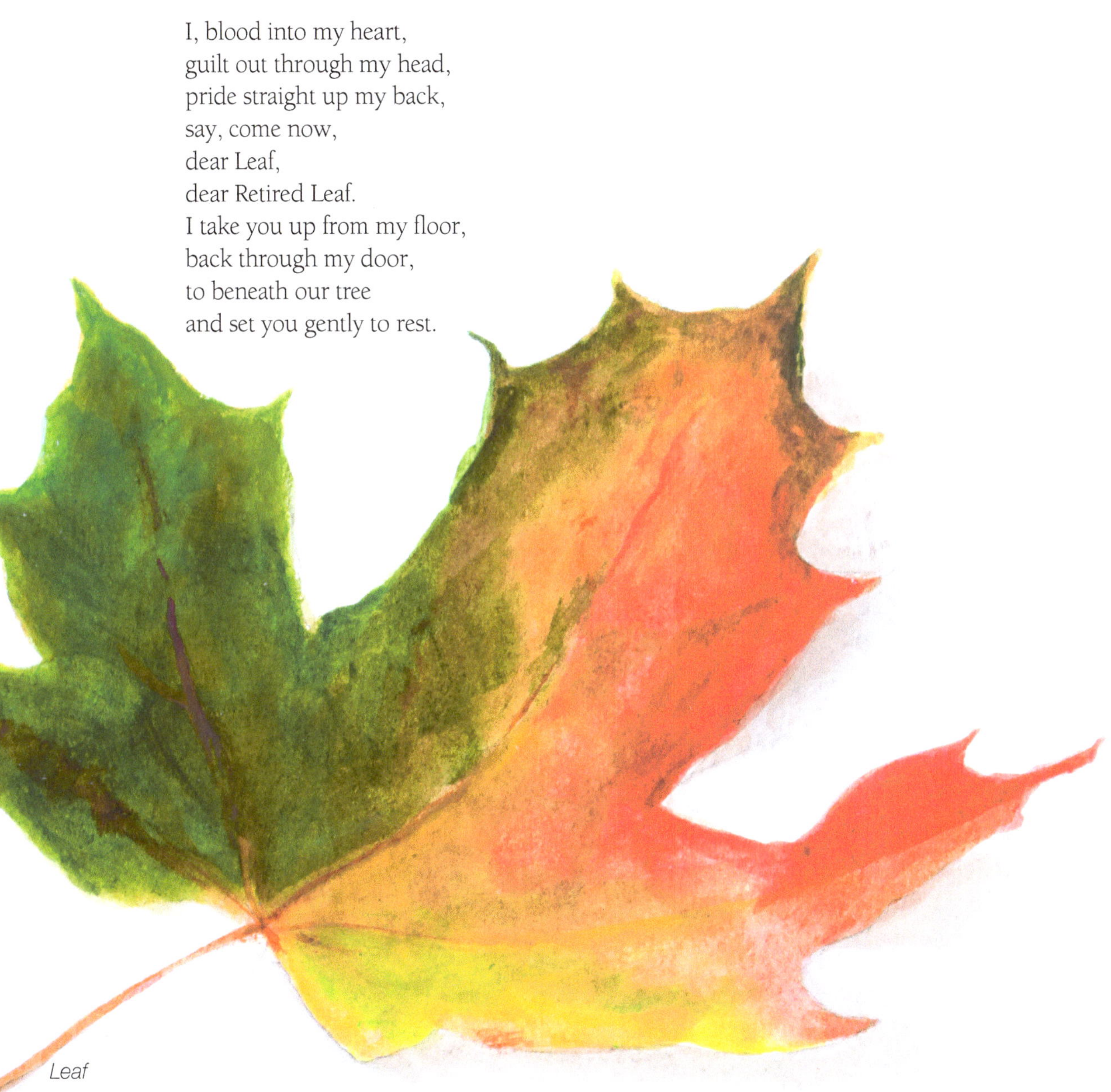

Leaf

Day of Success

Yesterday,
our day that started well,
ended better,
brought success
not perfection
but good enough to compensate for past delay.

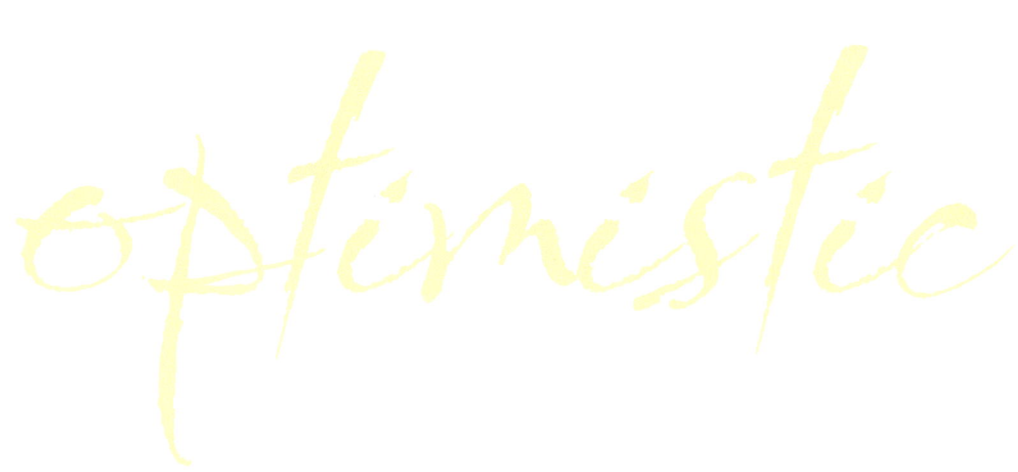

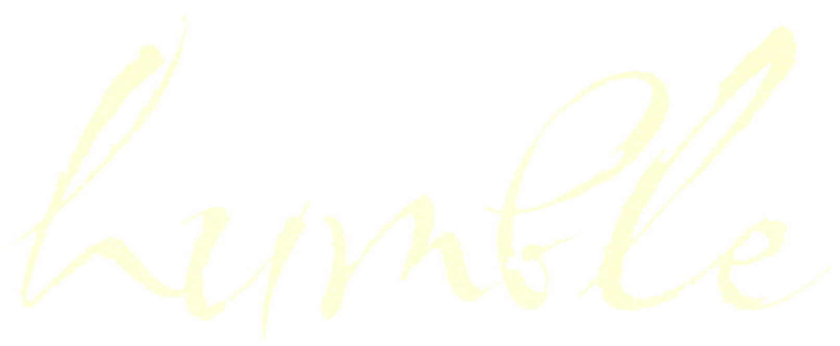

Today,
our day to glory
not worry,
but ponder why we chose to worry.

Success came as it had to come
by way of gift
we did not give
could not control,
could not expect,
but did accept
from others who assumed success
and (by their simple gift of faith)
made success
all
but
in-es-capable.

Tomorrow,
our day to try again
to be again
humble and optimistic.

Looks Forward and Backward

He walked,
crossed a bridge (rebuilt since falling to the flood)
turned down-creek
to that house of that friend who left today,
carried loaded boxes from basement to truck,
and worked till all were gone.
Again, he walked,
crossed a bridge (replaced since floating away)
and turned down-creek
to this house of this friend who will stay.
Now, he talks,
sips bowl of soup and cup of coffee,
looks forward to his way back,
looks backward to his way here,
speaks of each way as a good way,
and calls this day, a good day.

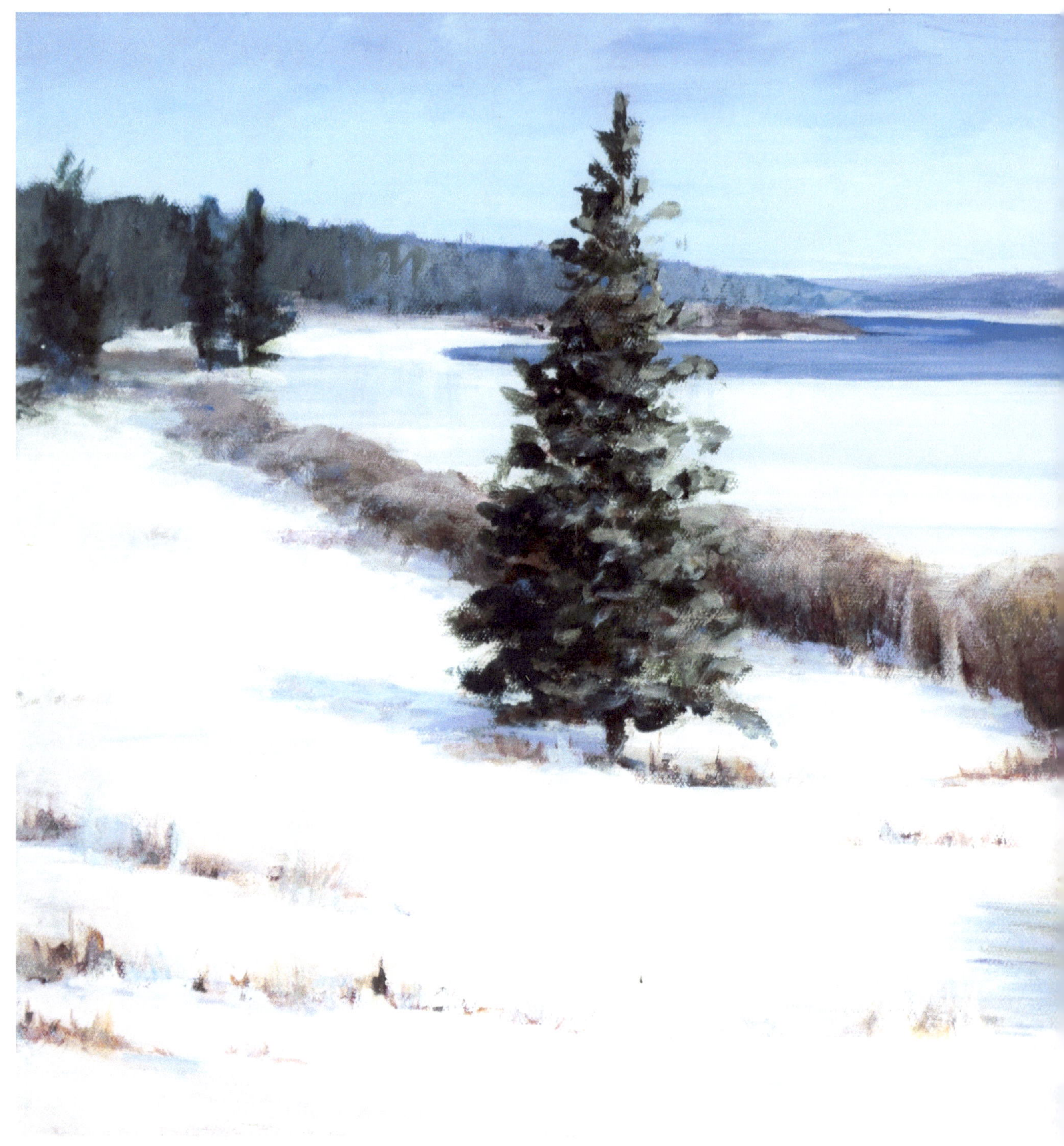

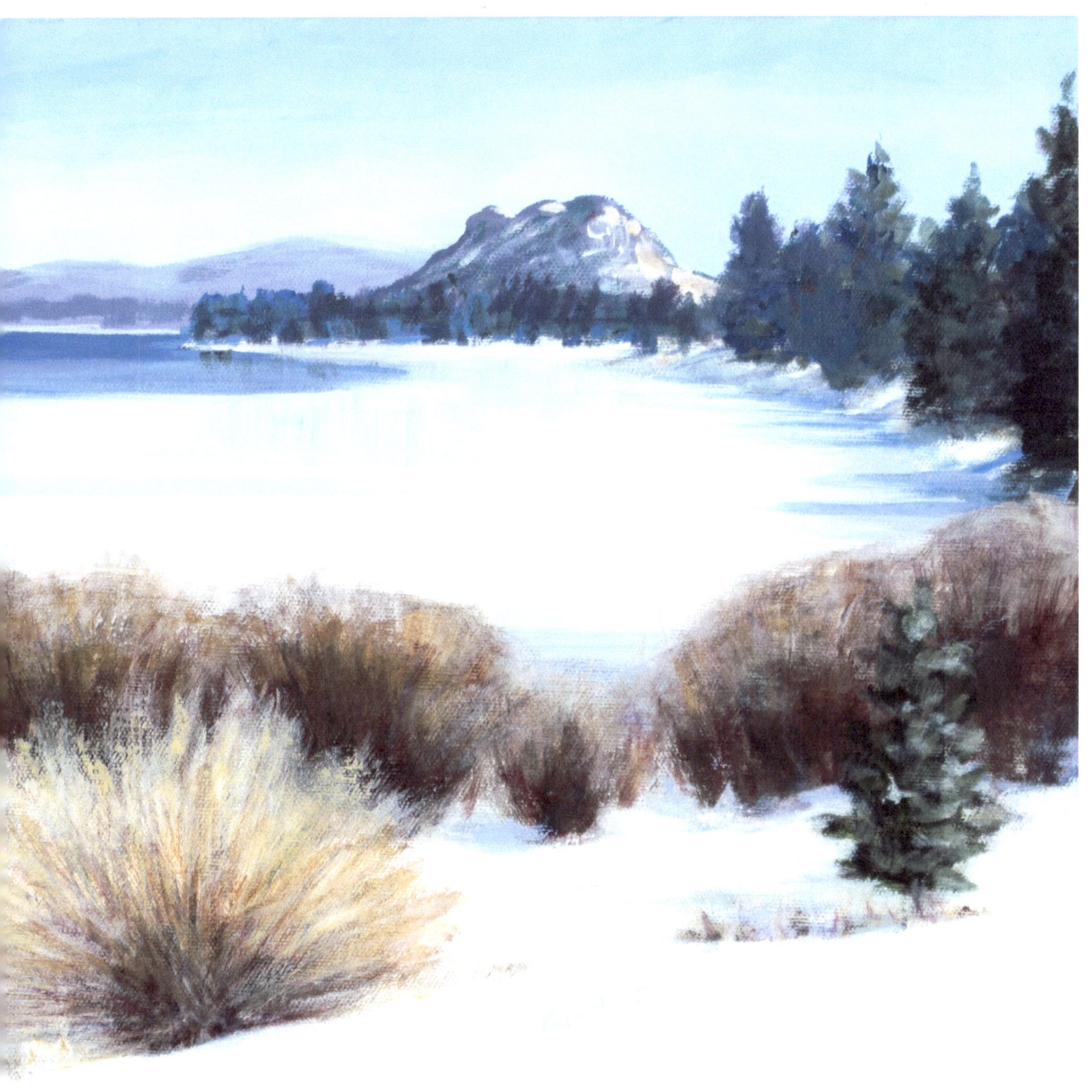

Pages 60–61: Parvin Lake Thaw

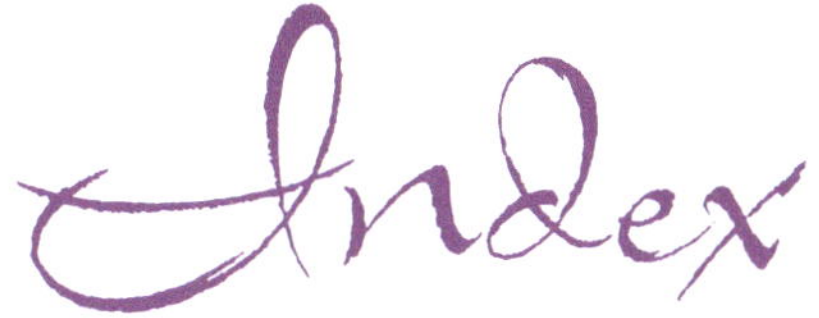

Winter

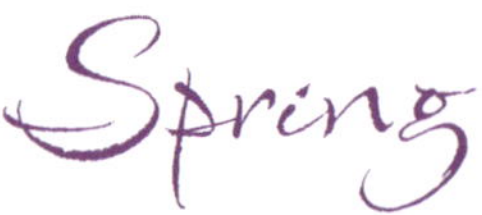

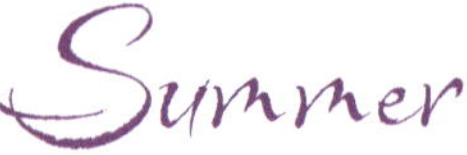

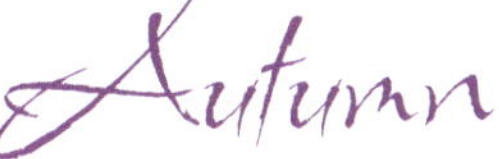

Afterword

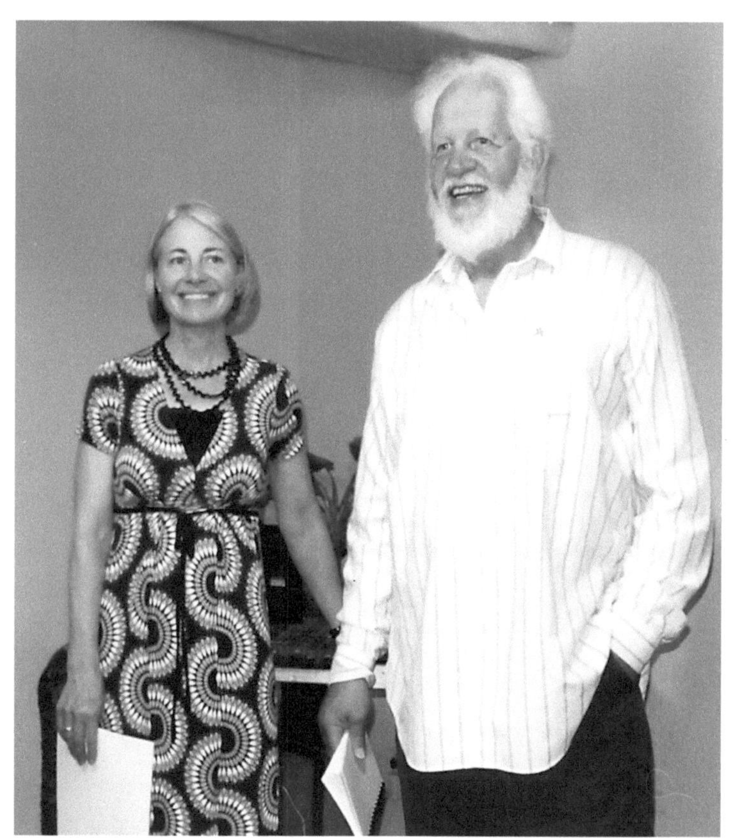
photo by Micah Richardson

Gale Whitman, artist

Discovering her gift for drawing while growing up in Kimball, Nebraska near the western edge of the Great Plain, Gale Whitman always wanted to be an artist. In school, however, she focused her studies on another interest, science—obtaining a bachelor of arts in biology and her master of science in anatomy/medical illustration. She explored her artistic path for ten years in Fort Collins as a professional medical illustrator. When her two children entered elementary school Gale took a deep breath, rented a studio, and returned to her art by venturing further into self expression. That venture has brought her several commissions within Fort Collins' public art programs and the opportunity to illustrate a children's book, *The Man From Space*—self-published with the story's author in 2012. Today Gale explores painting with acrylics, takes inspiration from nature and the human spirit, 'up-cycles' products she discovers in thrift shops, and acts as an Art in Public Places advocate. She and her family enjoy the riches that life in Fort Collins offers.

Bob Komives, poet

Bob started out near the eastern edge of the Great Plain in St. Paul, Minnesota. He came late to poetry, captivated always by place, people, and language: as land-use planner in New England, Colorado, and Central America; as a Peace Corps Volunteer who was so inspired by his struggle to master a second language that he spoke only Spanish to his now-multilingual daughters; as someone who learned Hungarian so he could better benefit from multiple explorations in the land of his paternal grandparents; as a cyclist who explores roads and towns near and far with his wife on their self-guided bicycle tours; and as one who always enjoys returning to life among his neighbors in Fort Collins. This life of good fortunes, of course, gives rise to diverse inspiration and joy as well as diverse concern and pain. Poetry is a medium for Bob to appreciate and express it all.

RPK Press
Komives-Whitman
324 East Plum Street
Fort Collins, CO 80524

www.GoodDayArtPoetry.com

www.ingramcontent.com/pod-product-compliance
Lightning Source LLC
LaVergne TN
LVHW070219110826
845147LV00003B/606

* 9 7 8 0 9 6 2 9 2 8 1 8 5 *